From the Library of
Lois J. Thomasson

Herbs Through the Seasons at Caprilands

Herbs Through the Seasons at Caprilands

Adelma Grenier
Simmons

photographs by
Randa Bishop

RODALE PRESS
Emmaus, PA

This book is meant to be educational in nature and is in no way meant to be used for self-treatment or self-diagnosis. Keep in mind that excess quantities of some herbs can be dangerous. The editors have attempted to include, wherever appropriate, cautions and guidelines for using the herbs and herbal recipes in this book. Yet, we realize that it is impossible for us to anticipate every conceivable use of herbs and every possible problem any use could cause. Moreover, we cannot know just what kinds of physical reactions or allergies some of you might have to substances discussed in this book.

For this reason, Rodale Press cannot assume responsibility for the effects of using the herbs or other information in his book. And we urge that all potentially serious health problems be managed by a physician.

For information, address: Rodale Press
33 East Minor Street, Emmaus, PA 18049

Photographs by Randa Bishop

Published by Rodale Press
33 East Minor Street, Emmaus, PA 18049

Editorial development and design by Combined Books
26 Summit Grove Avenue, Suite 207, Bryn Mawr, PA 19010

Produced by Wieser & Wieser
118 East 25th Street, New York, NY 10010

Library of Congress Cataloging-in-Publication Data

Simmons, Adelma Grenier.
Herbs through the seasons at Caprilands.

1. Herbs. 2. Herb gardening. 3. Herbs—Utilization.
4. Caprilands Herb Farm (Coventry, Conn.) 5. Cookery
(Herbs) I. Title.
SB351.H5S558 1987 635′.7′0974643 87-16556
ISBN 0-87857-727-0

Contents

AUTUMN

WINTER

I

Herbs Are Forever

Happy is the herb gardener through all the seasons and the years. That person enjoys a life enriched with rare fragrances at dawn and dusk and in the heat of noon. It is an esthetic experience to watch the patterns, textures, and shades of a gray-and-green garden develop through the changing seasons. The latent instinct for design is aroused by arranging muted tones and pleasing textures in garden rows, swirls, and knots. The householder's pride and pleasure can be satisfied in the rich harvest of green leaves and savory seeds for seasoning and in the everlasting foliage and blossoms for dried bouquets.

Spring, summer, autumn, and winter—all have added meaning, for to each season the garden yields a special taste and presents a picture quite its own. From the bleakness of early spring, when the pointed leaves of sorrel and the green spears of Egyptian onion pierce the frozen ground, to the richness of October when gray artemisias are ghostly signs against the autumn tapestry—and far into the winter—the herb garden continues. Long after the first frosts have destroyed summer's floral borders, coral-leafed santolinas, the wrinkled rosettes of horehound, and the woolly-soft lamb's-ears yield bouquets, wreaths, and swags to those who will walk in the cold of this melancholy season.

Fortunately the study of herbs touches all aspects of our lives, at all ages, under all conditions. What was a rigorous physical experience in youth and middle age may become an absorbing study for the armchair gardener who, halted in activities by age or physical handicap, can still enjoy a fascinating world of legend and history.

The textures and shades of gray and green in Caprilands dooryard garden give pleasure from dawn to dusk and through the changing seasons.

Caprilands Herb Farm covers fifty acres—some of it woodland.

Without moving far from a sunny windowsill or a cozy seat by the fire, you may plant an herb garden that knows no size, but may be as large or as small as your imagination reaches. In reality, you can derive hours of study and pleasure from a small collection of herbs grown in a window box, or a garden can be made outdoors in miniature—green and growing in a 24-inch circle. In the active days of youth, plan and plant your gardens, sow your seeds, and enjoy your harvests. Make seasonings, vinegars, mustards, jellies, decorations, potpourri, sweet jars, and pomanders tied with herbs of meaning. In later years, open up herbals and old garden books to study with amusement, tolerance, and not a little awe the wonderful history of herbs. Trace their uses from pagan ritual to Christian ceremony, their inclusion in early medicines, in witchcraft, in song and story until their enchantment lays a gentle hold on your daily life.

A Brief History of Caprilands Herb Farm

Caprilands Herb Farm in Coventry, Connecticut, is a place of special delight for people of all ages—those young enough to spend hours daily in rigorous gardening, as well as those who derive their pleasure from a garden in a window box or the appreciation of the history of herbs in books.

Caprilands is the realization of a dream . . . it is the re-creation of a very old, worn-out farm . . . of neglected land turned into production. It is the transformation of an area, once unsightly into a thing of beauty, our herb garden.

Fifty acres is ours, and all today, even the woodland, is serving some useful or aesthetic purpose.

In 1929, when my mother and father first saw Coventry, Silver Street, and the old house, then surrounded with the wreckage of years of mismanagement, it took imagination and not a little courage to visualize what it might become in the future.

In our family's first few years of residence, we concentrated on necessary restorations to make it habitable, and the development of the farm. Our original thought was to use our land for a small self-sustaining dairy farm with cattle, hens, pigs—a miniature of a Vermont farm (our home state). We even maintained a milk house, now our book shop, where we made our own butter and pot cheese. But we were absentee farmers, all with enviable jobs (in jobless 1929) and these could not be neglected. We found the Farm was one of those jobs, too, that couldn't be neglected, and could not run smoothly without daily owner attention. Temporarily we gave up the effort to dairy farm, and started instead to develop gardens. My own interest in herbs was superseded by an overwhelming desire to run a goat farm. This enterprise took up some years, and proved to be a fascinating

Adelma Simmons, middle, *has made Caprilands a center of activity based on herbs and herb lore.*

avocation, but was not a lucrative practice. Its chief legacies are remembered today in our name—Caprilands (or Goatlands).

I stood one day on the hill where our house is located and looked down on the level green area below, then the goat pasture, and suddenly saw it as the ideal herb garden. Broken stone walls enclosed it, green meadows rolled away from it, the woodland was distant enough to be a background without encroaching or shading. The land was stony, dry, unfertilized, but it had the two great essentials of the herb garden—sun and drainage. All we needed was time, labor, lime, a great idea, and most of all, the continuing enthusiasm to carry it on.

To develop this large plot as one garden was impossible without help and my own complete concentration, so I contented myself with one small patch which could be representative of the important herbs. This, in time, became the Butterfly Garden, named because of its form (not for any ability to attract butterflies). I laid the stone walks alone, and as I worked I dreamed of constructing a series of small plantings that would be harmonious together and would each depict some facet of herb growing. Each would be a complete garden in its own confines. The individual garden would also be a teaching medium, each one dramatizing some place in herbal garden history. The whole would be a living demonstration of planting, simple design, and appropriate accessories. It would be a living, natural workshop. As these plantings developed it became evident that much of this pasture, which had run wild, had to be kept under control; so large portions were mowed, others plowed and rototilled and seeded temporarily in unimaginative rows. This was necessary to supply the growing demand for herbs, and it prepared the ground for the eventual designed gardens, in the meantime giving the area a roughly finished look.

There were many interruptions to this long-term project, personal losses and sorrows which made it impossible to proceed with any great rapidity, but what a pleasure it was to turn from trouble to gardening, to work with the fragrant herbs, and to convert each garden plot into a little oasis of joy.

One by one the gardens grew, the cultivation and the maintenance factors became less appalling, and, in 1978, our original planned project was completed ending with the Potpourri and the Old Rose Garden. Since then we have added the Identification Garden. The dream itself has been realized, and the airy plans are at last a reality.

Caprilands Herb Farm is now the location of much daily activity based on herbs and herb lore. We enjoy our old house and gardens and all that goes with them. We try to present programs that are different, inspirational, educational, and fulfilling. In addition to our educational programs we offer tours, luncheons, greenhouses and shops where books, plants, and everything else associated with herbs may be purchased. It gives us great pleasure to share the delight of herbs with our guests.

The Herb Grower's World

Through the centuries in which man has explored and recorded his findings in the world of herbs, funds of information have widened and accumulated. Precious books are available for study in libraries, and some reprints of ancient volumes may be purchased at nominal prices.

The Saints Garden gives an aura of romantic legend to familiar plants.

Herb lore was collected by men and women in all walks of life—medicine men and sincere scholars can be contrasted with charlatans who snatched at every herbal straw to further their own fortunes; pious monks and monastic physicians, working with body as well as soul, opposed magicians and so-called witches who reveled in the dark world of ignorance and superstition.

Great poets like Virgil wrote about herbs, and peasants made memorable verses about them or told and retold tales that have become our folklore. Kings experimented with herbal medicines—even the august Charlemagne gave orders for the planting of herbs and vegeta-

bles. His is probably the must quoted definition of herbs: "The friend of the physician and the pride of cooks."

All of us, who study, write, or talk about herbs, or grow them, owe a debt to the past, for herbal history invests even our most unprepossessing plants with an aura of romantic legend. Quotations from herbals form part of most writers' material. The sayings of men like Dioscorides, Pliny the Elder, Nicholas Culpeper, and John Gerard are our precious heritage. Though their words are both fact and fancy, they give us a feeling of continuity and demonstrate the timelessness of herbal lore.

We do not stand alone in the wide world of herbs for there are many great gardeners there to keep us company—men like Francis Bacon, essayist, planner and planter of gardens for gentlemen, whose words I recall while walking through the reddening strawberry borders of my garden in fall, "Strawberry leaves dying yield a most cordial smell." William Lawson, who lived in the seventeenth century, took the country housewife's garden to heart, and today seems to whisper over our shoulder and advise, "Set slips in May and they grow aye." He also gives us a vision of his ideal garden that carries good advice and is charming to recall: "Large walks, broad and long, close and open like the Tempe groves in Thessaly, raised with gravel and sand, having seats

Knowledge of herbs common in gardens today was contained in precious scrolls and passed on by word of mouth for thousands of years.

and banks of camomile."

From this world of herbal information great names rise out of the mist of centuries. In days when there was little knowledge, these men studied and became sources of reference for their times. Brief notes about some of them are included here. (Such a short account must leave out some important names, and I hope you will forgive my omissions.)

The history of herbs starts five thousand years before the Christian era. The ancient Chaldeans, Chinese, Egyptians, and Assyrians had schools of herbalists. Their learning came in precious scrolls and by word of mouth through teachers, necromancers, and astrologers to the Greeks who through their philosophers and historians, particularly Aristotle and Plato, and their physicians Theophrastus and Hippocrates, advanced the use of herbs in literature, history, and medicine.

It was in the first century that Dioscorides became famous in botany and medicine. A Greek from Asia Minor, he traveled with the Roman legions, probably as an army doctor. He studied the healing herbs of the world he knew and recorded his findings in *Materia Medica,* which dealt with more than five hundred plants. His original work was destroyed, but a Byzantine copy dated about 512 A.D. survived the

In Benedictine cloisters daily garden work was considered an important part of religious life. Today herb gardeners find similar solice in simple chores such as weeding.

years and has been studied in facsimile by many generations. In the sixteenth and seventeenth centuries Dioscorides was the most widely read of all authors. His popularity was due in part to the enlargement of the work by Pierandrea Mattioli who also embellished the text with magnificent woodcuts. A condensed edition of this work is available today and makes fascinating reading.

Pliny the Elder, a contemporary of Dioscorides, wrote of many things in his *Natural History*—both the practical and the fabulous. Through his pages roam birds, animals, and plants that never were: there are cures that surely must have killed; and magic parades as science, accepted and practiced for generations. Pliny met his death in the destruction of Pompeii, refusing to leave his research, his books, and home. My volumes of Pliny are old, hard to read, and falling to pieces, but they are so filled with interest and discoveries that I feel time with them is well spent.

After Pliny the succeeding centuries brought us the period of monastic herbals. The cultivation of plants in the quiet world of the cloister produced many treatises on growing herbs and vegetables. The Benedictine Rule included daily work and gardening as important in the religious life. Plans of the monastery of St. Gall still present a

Herbals of the sixteenth and seventeenth centuries contained long lists of plants; in them are named the plants of our gardens today, such as St. Barbara's Cress.

graphic record of the period.

It is in the sixteenth and seventeenth centuries that we come to the English herbals that are best known and most frequently quoted. Here the names of Bancke (1525), *The grete herball* (1526), and Turner (1568) lead us to the most quoted herbal of all, John Gerard's *The Herball or Generall Historie of Plantes,* published in 1597. Gerard was a barber-surgeon whose greatest interest was gardening. Fashionable Holborn in England was the place where he cultivated the long list of plants that furnished subject matter for his pen and a garden for the study, wonder, and admiration of his contemporaries. While the years and advance of science may have taken some luster from Gerard's name (his tall tales of "trees bearing geese" and the "Barnakle tree" can scarcely be credited as scientific accounts), he is still read for many truths that bear repeating. His book is richly illustrated. Much of its content was drawn from a manuscript left by a Dr. Priest whose work was not acknowledged. Gerard was condemned by a later publisher, but his own abilities were so great that no ancient accusation has been able to change his standing. Sometimes to forget the awfulness of the atom, I follow his advice. "Who would therefore looke dangerously up at Planets, that might safely looke down at Plants?"

John Parkinson was herbalist to Charles I and is remembered for a book published in 1629 called *Paradisi in Sole Paradisus Terrestris.* Later he produced a much larger work called the *Theatrum botanicum: the theatre of plants, or, an herball of a large extent.*

Astrology and the herbalist have ever seemed to go together, but in the seventeenth century the vogue of tying each herb to a star was at its height and Nicholas Culpeper (1616–1654) made the most of the fad. He established a practice as astrologer and physician at Spitalfields and caused great indignation among medical men of his day by publishing *A Physicall Directory,* an unauthorized translation of the *Pharmacopoeia* issued by the College of Physicians. In spite of, or perhaps because of, the controversies that Culpeper caused, he became the most popular writer of his day and still finds enthusiastic readers. His herbals went into many editions and often appear in old bookshops.

Spring

The Blue Garden has lavender blooming in the spring.

Fresh herbs are creatively constructed into decorative items.

A Caprilands gardener handles a young plant with care as he unpots it in preparation for planting.

A profusion of flowers covers a Caprilands salad.

A simple serving of soup is brightened by a calendula.

Several shops greet visitors to Caprilands.

Morris dancers romp around the May Pole on a warm spring day.

Two friends go for a stroll outside a greenhouse.

II

Spring Diary

He who sees things grow from the beginning will have the best view of them.
—*ARISTOTLE*

There is always one morning in late March or early April when I bundle up and go trudging off in search of spring. There's still a bite in the air and the wind is hardly gentle, but I am tired of fireside planning and ready for the doing.

Here and there I lift the salt hay cover to see how my low-growing herbs have fared. I look under the mulch on the banks of creeping thyme and the hedges of *Thymus vulgaris.* I check the compost around the santolinas. A spring thaw can leave even these fairly hardy herbs bare and vulnerable. As the morning sun warms the air a little, I tamp down a rootlet, firm the slightly heaving soil around the horehound, lift a Christmas tree bough to inspect my germanders, even though I know it is too soon to expect even a greening leaf. I push aside the leaf cover on the lavender bed to find the marker and go off to the shed for a bigger one. Early weeding could easily destroy the seedlings here for it will be mid-June before they show up.

For me, it's spring now; my mind is filled with things to do; I've pots of well-started plants to go out when it's warm enough and stacks of notes on what to do and when—and why. Before long, daylight hours will be all too short. My hands are aching for the touch of warm soil, and my eyes are ready for the greens and yellows of spring after winter's browns and grays. As I walk back to the house I know that very soon there'll be no time to dream over a cup of tea.

All gardeners are anxious to transfer well-started plants into the sunshine on warm spring days.

III

Planting the Herb Garden

This rule in gardening never forget,
To sow dry and set wet.
—OLD PROVERB

It is fine to have a perfect location for your herb garden, but if this is not possible, don't worry needlessly. Here at Caprilands where I have five acres of lawn and planting (and 50 acres of woodland and meadows), the gardens are not all ideally placed. The Saints Garden, our meditation spot, private and secluded on level but not well-drained land, gets little sun. This is a challenge, but, fortunately, there is an herb for every location and favorites will grow to some extent under trying conditions.

The "perfect" site for an herb garden is well-drained, with a slight slope so that water does not linger around the crowns of plants. A neutral to slightly alkaline or sweet soil is best for most herbs. If your soil is acid and azaleas and rhododendrons thrive, apply generous amounts of limestone to the herb garden each spring. The third requisite is sun. Herbs profit by eight hours of sunshine daily in summer, but if your grounds are shady, you can still grow herbs, although they will grow taller than usual, and those you plant for seasoning will have less flavor.

A secluded garden provides an ideal spot for meditation.

Brick walkways are an invitation to stroll in a garden, no matter what the weather.

How to Prepare the Ground

After you select the site, stake out boundaries. Remove any large rocks, other debris, and small underbrush or weeds. Work up the soil to a depth of 12 inches, using a tiller or spade. As you come upon stones, sticks, and bits of wood, collect and remove them, too. If witchgrass is present, as it is here, sift out every last white root you can find.

I recommend three rototillings or diggings: the first to remove the sticks and stones; the second to incorporate well-rotted compost or well-decayed cow manure in soil lacking humus; the third to mix in the garden lime spread on top until the ground is nearly white. Where soil is strongly acid, allow 100 pounds of lime for a garden 12 by 18 feet. Even sweet woodruff, lovage, and angelica will tolerate lime, and thymes, lavenders, and santolinas can't live without it. If mints have enough moisture, they seem to be able to grow well in any soil. Therefore, except in areas where the soil is already neutral or on the alkaline side (pH 7.0 or higher), it is wise to apply lime to the herb garden every second or third year in late winter or early spring.

To Put Your Plan into Action

First drive a stake at each corner of the outside boundaries of your herb garden, making the area a few inches larger than you want it to be when completed. Stretch a sturdy cord taut from one stake to the other until the garden is fenced in. Then, with a steel tape measure and more

Sturdy cord stretched between stakes outlines straight edges for planting beds and walks.

stakes and string, measure off and outline the beds with flour or lime. I sketch in the curving lines with the thin, long blade of a tobacco hoe and true them afterward. Next, lay walks of whatever material you prefer—old brick, native fieldstone, wood chips, or even grass. In a contemporary setting, bricks might be used for the walkways with redwood frames rising 2 or 3 inches above the ground to outline each herb bed. This works well if beds have only straight lines, but it is impractical with curves.

Now you are ready to plant. Generally hardy perennial herbs are bought as plants, the biennials and annuals started each year from seeds. If your budget is limited, buy just two each of the perennial herbs you want. As these grow, you can divide or propagate by cuttings. Order your herb plants by mail or visit a nursery as early in the season as possible, so you will be sure to get the kinds you want.

Herbs from Seeds

I find that all herb seeds do better if they are started outdoors where fresh air, full light, and coolness promote vigorous growth. I have tried raising plants in the greenhouse, transferring them later to coldframes

Seedlings in pots grow on benches outside one of the Caprilands greenhouses.

for hardening off, but this is hazardous. Often plants started from seeds sown outside are as large as those started earlier in the greenhouse.

The business of planting seeds should be a simple process, as natural as nature. For some reason gardeners like to make a ritual of sterilizing soil, and performing light test, soil tests, and germination tests with all the protocol of the laboratory. In fact, I know many gardeners who get so wound up in all this that they never get around to the actual sowing of the seeds.

When frost danger is past and you have spaded or tilled the soil until it is in mellow, friable condition, you are ready to sow seeds. Mark out the rows with a hoe, making them wide enough to do a little scattering. Sprinkle the seeds over the prepared area, scatter soil lightly over them, then moisten with a misty spray of water from the hose. The seeds will probably germinate if you do not cover them, but sharp-sighted birds often pick up many of their favorite coriander, caraway, and other seeds if these are left uncovered at planting time. The general rule is to cover seeds to a depth that is three times their thickness. If seeds are dust-size, merely press them into the planting medium. I usually sow seeds like this in a protected coldframe outdoors, or in a flat or bulb pan inside, as described later in this chapter.

After sowing your seeds, do not be impatient; some herbs are slow to germinate. Generally, they seem to do better if you don't watch over them too anxiously. But it is important to keep the seeded area reasonably moist until germination is well along. If the weather is cool and wet, no special care is needed, but as the season advances it helps to stretch burlap, tobacco or cheesecloth across the seed rows to keep the soil evenly moist. If you do this, be sure that this cover is removed by the time seedlings show above the ground.

I learned long ago to sow all my seeds at one time. First sowings, particularly very early ones, are often washed out in heavy spring rains, or destroyed by unseasonable cold. When this happens, you will want a second sowing.

My own seed-planting methods are not exactly meticulous, but I get good results. For the gardener with a few packets of seeds to sow instead of several pounds, a more cautious method is probably desirable. Prepare the soil carefully, screen out clods and stones, level by raking, then soak with water. When the soil has dried enough to be workable, make drills to the depth of a pencil point and sprinkle the seeds in these, spacing as evenly as possible, Cover lightly, firm the soil, keep moist, and good germination should be the result.

Sometimes in the creation of an herb garden you can use free-form clumps or groupings of each kind of plant instead of straight rows. You can mark off these spaces inside a bed with the edge of a hoe and redraw them until the effect is pleasing. Then start your planting, broadcasting the seeds of each plant in the area chosen for it.

In shaped beds herbs have a more pleasing effect planted in clumps rather than rows.

After hardening off, seedlings of sufficient size can be planted in the garden.

Time for sowing varies from one area to another. Your county agent in the county court house represents the United States Department of Agriculture, and has up-to-date average dates for the last killing frosts in your locality. It is generally safe to sow all seeds after that date. Here, in New England, I try thyme, rosemary, lavender, hyssop, rue, sweet marjoram, savory, parsley, chervil, chives, calendula, bachelor's-button, caraway, and coriander on the fifteenth of April. I always gamble and plant a few basil seeds then, although I know they are sensitive to cold and will not germinate until the weather is warm. Once in a while April in Connecticut turns out to be warm enough for the first-planted basils to produce an early crop that delights me.

Early planting of herbs is not vital to success. There are many that grow well from seeds sown in summer. I always put in a second planting of basil in early July. I sow burnet seeds as soon as they ripen in order to have small seedlings for potting. Thyme, dill, and parsley are others that may be sown in summer. August-sown seeds provide seedlings for transplanting into winter window boxes.

Herb Seeds Indoors

If you have to have plants early, start them in February or March in the sunniest and coolest window you have, or under fluorescent lights. Annuals to try early inside include basil, summer savory, sweet marjoram, dill, parsley, chervil, and calendula.

For this early planting, use flats or boxes, or bulb pans filled with a mixture of 2 parts sand and 1 part vermiculite. Moisten well, then sow the seeds and barely cover them. Keep in a well-lighted place and water from the bottom as often as necessary to keep the surface soil evenly moist. As soon as germination starts, move containers into the sun. When seedlings are large enough to handle, transplant them to pots filled with a mixture of equal parts vermiculite, garden loam, and compost (or peat moss if you do not have compost). The seedlings need a nighttime temperature of 50 to 60 degrees and plenty of fresh air in the daytime.

As spring approaches and days get warm, harden off the seedlings started indoors by sinking the small pots down in the soil of a coldframe until they take on a healthy outdoor look. Or you can group the seed flats, boxes, or pots on a protected porch for a few days. After this hardening off, the seedlings will be ready for planting directly in the garden.

If you are sowing dust-fine seeds of herbs, such as pennyroyal, ambrosia, or wormwood, half fill a pot with good potting soil and cover with screened sphagnum moss or vermiculite. Moisten, then sow seeds over the surface, thinly and evenly. Don't press in or cover with soil, but place the pot inside a polyethylene bag or cover with a pane of glass. Either will retain moisture so that the fine seeds will sprout. As soon as they show vigorous growth, remove plastic or glass, at first just for an hour or two, gradually increasing the time until the seedlings are hardened off and no covering is necessary.

Perennial Herbs from Seeds

Perennial herbs that grow easily from seeds include hyssop, salad burnet, chives, fennel, pennyroyal, rue, sage, sweet marjoram, *Majorana hortensis,* and thyme *(Thymus vulgaris).* If you have patience and a place to start them where they can remain undisturbed, try the more difficult lemon balm, catnip, horehound, lavender, lovage, mint, rosemary, winter savory, sweet woodruff, and wormwood. Sweet cicely grows best from self-sown seeds in the place where it is established. Herbs best propagated by division of roots or from stem cuttings include tarragon, angelica, most artemisias, santolina, germander, most mints, and rosemary. True tarragon for seasoning can't be grown from seed. Rosemary and lavender are really slow and unreliable germinators.

Tarragon grows in profusion around bottles of vinegar containing cuttings. Tarragon for seasoning can't be grown from seed.

A lavender flower stalk is a natural attraction for bees.

Lavender from Seeds

Lavender seeds are notoriously slow to germinate, sometimes taking six months. Coolness seems to be an essential condition for bringing this seed out. For many years I was determined to grow lavender from seeds. I bought them from many firms in many parts of the world. Occasionally I was rewarded with a single weak plant, but never with any result commensurate with the time and effort put into the project.

One autumn I dropped a season's accumulation of lavender seed packets in a row in the garden where, except for cleaning away the leaves, no weeding is done until the first of June. The next spring I found a small forest of seedlings, so tiny they did not resemble lavender, but I had only to touch them to get the wonderful lavender odor. The seedlings grew undisturbed until they were large enough to be transplanted. Later these plants became the wide lavender border that leads to our side entrance in the dooryard garden, as well as part of our new Lavender Garden.

Now I always grow lavender from seeds sown in November, with sometimes another sowing in March. *Lavandula spica* is the most certain and quickest to germinate, but the plants are generally not very hardy or long lived; they are well worth growing however, for the fragrant white foliage. Blossoms are borne on stems sometimes 2 feet tall, pale in color, and not as sweet as *Lavendula vera* and its varieties.

IV

Herbs Are Good Companions

Caprilands gardens started forty-five years ago. At that time few gardeners (none that I knew) gave any thought to companion plants. Everything planted in those first few years grew exceedingly well. The garden was very small, just a dooryard patch, so plants were very near together. The rue, along with the basil and fennel, flourished without any noticeable inhibiting of other plants. There were few insects and no troubles. However, as the years went on, we extended our gardens into new areas and felt that we were tempting predators who always seem to be happier with large spaces devoted to one solid planting. Our decision to interplant vegetables (only small salad types) meant that we would be attracting other predators, for many that did not attack herbs would find the vegetables delectable. All these elements were instrumental in the decision to do companion planting.

The ideas behind companion planting are that many common garden pests find being in the vicinity of certain common plants repugnant, and certain common plants grow better near other plants. We came to our experiment in companion planting without much conviction. I did not believe in many of the popular ideas, and some I still do not accept after trying out different theories over a period of years.

The plan of our garden opens from a central walk 50 feet long. It is made of field stone from partially demolished old stone walls. On either side of the walk is a permanent border of strawberries, which are

Companion planting is based on the idea that some plants repel pests that are attracted to other plants.

charming and disease-free and provide leaves for medicinal tea. In back of the strawberries are pot marigolds and behind them is a long row of sage. The sage repels the cabbage butterfly and so keeps the cabbages in that area free of that pest. Tubs of rosemary nearby are reputed to grow better near the sage. We plant valerian near the vegetables because it is thought to attract the invaluable earthworm. And so, throughout our companion garden we have planted herbs interspersed with vegetables so that one plant benefits from the proximity to others.

Here is a partial listing of herbs that are good companions. You may wish to conduct your own experiments with them and test the value of their relationships.

ANISE *(Pimpinella anisum)*—Annual—Plant from seed, sow early, harvest as seeds are ripe. Strong scent, bug free, friendly to coriander, other seed herbs.

BALM, Lemon *(Melissa officinalis)*—Perennial—Tea herb, strong smelling, bug free.

These basil seedlings are ready to be thinned.

BASIL *(Ocimum basilicum)*—Annual—Friendly to all in the garden. Plant with tomatoes.

BORAGE *(Borago officinalis)*—Annual—Grow from seed. Aids growth, adds flavor, protects strawberries.

BROOM (*Genista* species)—Perennial Shrub—for calcium in soil. Reputed to grow best with lavender.

CALENDULA *(Calendula officinalis)*—Annual—Grow from seeds sown early. Deters asparagus beetles, tomato worms and other garden pests.

CARAWAY *(Carum carvi)*—Biennial—Plant with anise, plant from seed, harvest second year. Foliage is strong smelling, bug repellent.

CASTOR BEAN *(Ricinus communis)*—Annual—Spurge family, eradicates plant lice, repels moles. Grow from seed, grows very large, plant at end of rows. Seeds are poisonous.

CHIVES *(Allium schoenoprasum)*—Perennial—Plant as borders.

DATURA *(Datura stramonium)*—Perennial—Japanese beetles dislike it. Warning: seeds are poison if eaten.

Several pests can be controlled by planting marigolds near vegetables.

DEAD NETTLE (*Lamium* species)—Perennial—Deters potato bugs, improves growth and flavor.

DILL *(Anethum graveolens)*—Annual—Plant seeds or small seedlings, make successive sowings. Plant with coriander, caraway and anise throughout the garden.

FLAX (*Linum* species)—Annual and Perennial—Plant both perennial and annual, for potato bug extermination. Blue flowers, very attractive.

GARLIC *(Allium sativum)*—Perennial—To protect roses from rose bugs, aphids and Japanese beetles.

GERANIUM (*Pelargonium* species and cultivars) white or scented geraniums—Perennial—To rid garden of Japanese beetles, insects dislike them.

HYSSOP *(Hyssopus officinalis)*—Perennial—Plant near grapes, use as a tea for plant bacteria.

LAVENDER *(Lavendula officinalis)*—Perennial—A moth preventative. Bug free.

LOVAGE *(Levisticum officinale)*—Perennial—Strong celery-smelling plant. Bug repellent.

MARIGOLDS (*Tagetes* varieties)—Annual—Improves soil, controls nematodes, root diseases, bean beetles.

NASTURTIUM (Tropaeolum species)—Annual—Controls aphids, white fly, striped beetle, squash bug, woolly aphids.

NETTLES *(Urtica dioica)*—Perennial—Increases flavor and taste of surrounding plants, essential oils, stimulates rich humus formation, rich in iron and vitamins, use as a mulch. Plant near broccoli. Early spring salad green.

ONIONS (*Allium* species)—Perennial and Annual—Interspersed with plants—thought to repel rabbits.

PARSLEY *(Petroselinum crispum)*—Biennial—Grow with tomatoes.

PENNYROYAL *(Mentha pulegium)*—Tender Perennial—Repels ants, fleas and flies.

PEPPERMINT *(Mentha piperita)*—Perennial—Strong smelling, bug repellent, repels mice and rats, put in runs. Use as a tea.

PETUNIA (*Petunia* varieties)—Annual—Plant with beans for protection from pests.

ROSEMARY *(Rosmarinus officinalis)*—Perennial—Plant with sage. Wards off the cabbage worm, bean beetle.

RUE *(Ruta graveolens)*—Perennial—Repels horseflies and house flies, aphids, blackfly. Medicinal. Leaves may give rash to some people.

Dill makes a flavorful vinegar.

Above left, *rosemary is said to control cabbage worms and bean beetles.*

Above right, *summer savory is used in cooking beans and onion dishes.*

SAGE *(Salvia officinalis)*—Perennial—Plant with rosemary, for carrots, peas, broccoli, Brussels sprouts.

SOUTHERNWOOD *(Artemisia abrotanum)*—Perennial—Moth repellent, enemy to cabbage worms and harmful butterflies.

SPEARMINT *(Mentha spicata)*—Perennial—Repels ants, aphids, rodents and the flea beetle.

STRAWBERRY (*Fragaria* species)—Perennial—Plant near spinach and borage.

SUMMER SAVORY—*(Satureja hortensis)*—Plant with beans, repels the bean beetle. Use in cooking with beans, onions.

TANSY *(Tanacetum vulgare)*—Perennial—Controls ants, aphids, flies, fleas, moths, Japanese beetles. Good for compost, leaves for moth preventative.

TARRAGON *(Artemisia dracunculus)*—Perennial—repels insects.

THYME *(Thymus vulgaris)*—Enlivens other plants in the garden, repels cabbage worms.

VALERIAN *(Valeriana officinalis)*—Perennial—Attracts earthworms, helps vegetables, makes a spray for health of plants.

WORMWOOD *(Artemisia absinthium)*—Perennial—For fleas, slug extermination, cabbage fly, black flea beetle, repels small animals. Use as a spray with care on young seedlings.

YARROW *(Achillea millefolium)*—Perennial—Increases the aromatic quality of all herbs, helps vegetables.

V

The Versatile Thymes

For he painted the things that matter,
The tints that we all pass by,
Like the little blue wreaths of incense
That the wild thyme breathes to the sky;
Or the first white bud of the hawthorne,
And the light in a blackbird's eye;
—*ALFRED NOYES*

Literature is filled with references to thyme—hillsides, banks, and mounds of thyme; old sundials surrounded with thyme in pleasant symbolism; thyme that smells like "dawn in Paradise" and thyme with its clean fragrance in the manger hay at Bethlehem. There are walks and alleys of thyme, and old-time gardens with thyme lawns and terraces. There are upright thymes to make little hedges in a culinary garden, and dark green, glossy-leaved kinds cherished for their exquisite lemon odor. There is a thyme as gray as a lichen-covered rock and another that appears to be covered with yellow flowers, but it is the leaves that are touched with gold. There is a silver-variegated thyme, too. Varieties are legion, and many defy classification. Every thyme-filled garden is likely to have at least one that is an unnamed gift of nature.

Legend surrounds thyme with pleasant symbolism.

About the Name

For plants as common as thyme there are usually many common names, but for thyme there are few and *Thymum* has almost sufficed through centuries for these interesting little plants found throughout the temperate zone, in the Azores, Corsica, England, France, Italy, and Russia. The greatest number, including commercial types from which the essential oil thymol is distilled, grow along mountainous shores of the Mediterranean on dry rocks under burning sun.

In a treatise on the plants of Shakespeare, Canon Ellacombe notes that early English vocabularies do not include the word thyme in its present form. A vocabulary of the thirteenth century lists "Epitime, epithimum, fordboh," and this may be the wild thyme. In the fifteenth century thyme appears as *Hoc sirpillum.* Gerard spells thyme "time," and this reminds us that it was once called "punning thyme" because of its association with passing hours and the fact that it is difficult not to make a pun when speaking of thyme.

Several plants not true thymes bear the names "basil thyme" and "cat thyme." In the time of Theophrastus, savories and thymes were classed together, and the old names cling. Perhaps also any small, strong-smelling plant might once have been given the name of this widely distributed family. Thus oregano is often called Greek thyme, though it is *Origanum vulgare.*

In Europe these small fragrant and aromatic thymes were symbols of energy and activity. To insure his success in battle, the medieval lady embroidered a bee hovering over a sprig of thyme on the scarf she presented to her knight, and young girls used thyme with mint and lavender in a nosegay to bring them sweethearts. Little bushes of thyme were planted on graves, particularly in Wales, and sprigs of thyme were often carried by secret orders like the Odd Fellows at funerals to be dropped into the graves.

According to tradition, thyme was in the hay and straw bed of Virgin Mary and the Christ Child. It is therefore one of the "manger herbs" to be included in the nativity scene.

The wild thyme belongs to pastures, rocky promontories, and the valleys of the Alps but it also thrives along roadsides, in walks, and borders. It is so vigorous that less bold and invasive herbs must be protected from its encroachment. Breathing in its heady scent, we understand why the ancients believed that where the wild thyme grew, the atmosphere was purified as well as perfumed.

A pleasant summer sound is the hum of bees above a flowering bank of thyme. It is truly the bees' plant, for with the first blooms in May the bee chorale starts, low and controlled. By late June, with the

At Caprilands bee hives are located in the herb gardens.

hillside a mass of pink and purple blossoms the hum rises to a fine frenzy. Then the honey gatherers are so thick that I garden in early morning or after sunset to avoid them.

Classic writers tell of the bees and wild plants that covered Mount Hymettus. Then, thyme was a symbol of sweetness, and Virgil, beekeeper as well as poet, wrote, "Thyme, for the time it lasteth, yieldeth most and best honni and therefore in old time was accounted chief. . . . Hymettus in Greece and Hybla in Sicily were so famous for bees and honni, because there grew such store of thyme."

In parts of England wild thyme is called shepherd's thyme, and it was once thought to bring illness into a house, a contradiction of the belief that thyme cured melancholy.

Virtues of Thyme

Gerard wrote, "It [thyme] helpeth against the bitings of any venomous beast, either taken in drinke, or outwardly applied." And Culpeper reported: "[*Thymus vulgaris*] is a strengthener of the lungs, a good remedy for the chin cough in children. It purges the blood of phlegm and is an excellent remedy for the shortness of breath. . . . gives safe and speedy delivery to women in travail. . . . an ointment made of it takes away hot swellings and warts. . . . helps sciatica and dullness of sight. . . . is excellent for those troubled with gout. . . . taken inwardly comforts the stomach much, and expells wind. . . . And infusion of the leaves of *Thymus serpyllum* removes headaches

A traditional beekeep adds nostalgia to the herb garden.

occasioned by inebriation and is excellent for nervous disorders. A strong infusion tea—a very effectual remedy for headache, giddiness, and a certain remedy for that troublesome complaint, the nightmare."

Wild thyme has been used in an infusion as a remedy for flatulence, also in the treatment of coughs and sore throat. Culpeper wrote, "If you make a vinegar of the herb as vinegar of roses is made and anoint the head with it, it presently stops the pain thereof. It is very good to be given either in frenzy or lethargy."

To make a tea of wild thyme, mix 3 parts dried thyme with 1 part each of dried rosemary and spearmint. Store in a tightly closed teapot; infuse 1 teaspoon to 1 cup water. Let brew at least 10 minutes; serve hot; I find the tea excellent for headaches and to calm nerves; it is said to be useful also in warding off colds and fevers.

To make thyme vinegar, remove a third of the liquid from a quart bottle of white distilled vinegar, then fill with the trimmings of thyme, stems and all. Store in a warm place for a month. The vinegar is then useful as a sun-tanning lotion in the summer, and, when rubbed on the skin, it will drive away insects. Useful also in the treatment of insect bites and bee stings. And, of course, it is an excellent basis for a salad dressing.

Oil of thyme is sometimes used as a counter-irritant in rheumatism. Obtained by the distillation of fresh leaves and flowering tops, this oil, first discovered in Germany in 1725 by an apothecary to the Court of Berlin, was then given the name, "thymol." It is a powerful antiseptic mainly for external use as a lotion, also as a salve for ringworm and burns.

Thymes planted in orchards where blossoms attract bees assure good pollination of fruit. If the trees are small and trim so that the thymes beneath them get adequate air and sun, the effect is delightful. The thought of flowering fruit trees and fragrant mats of thyme puts me in tune with those ancient scholars who not only were gardeners and agriculturists, but writers who told of their discoveries and experiments in verse and prose that I find inspiring today.

How to Plant Thyme

Thymes need sun and good drainage, alkaline or sweet soil. Rocks for plants to clamber over are also near-requisites. Thymes will exist, though hardly thrive, on a terrace that receives bright, strong light all day, or direct sun half the day. My variety 'Caprilands' grows well on a terrace that faces northwest, a location heavily shaded until midday but exposed to afternoon sun. In my small Biblical garden, the paths of thyme that form a cross have done well although the area is surrounded by trees and gets only filtered sun all day, with direct sun for about two hours.

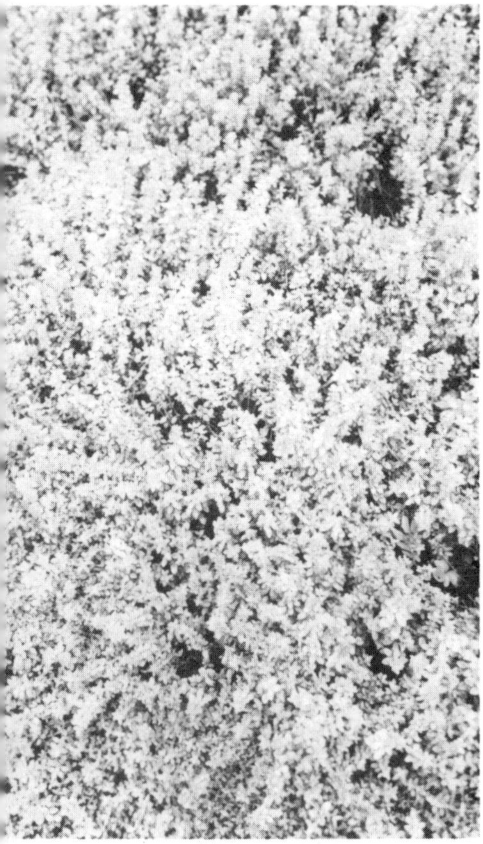

Golden thyme is one variety grown at Caprilands.

When you plant thyme, be sure its roots are well down in the soil. Otherwise they may work up and be burned by the sun before they take hold. When planting between stones in a walk or terrace, make a pocket for the roots, water the soil well, and bury the plant till only one-third of it is exposed. If you do this in warm weather, cover the transplant with burlap until it is established, lifting the cover only for long periods of rain or damp, humid weather. When you remove the burlap for good, mulch the soil around the roots with grass clippings or buckwheat hulls.

Thyme from Seed

Pliny the Elder wrote, "For the sake of honey we have brought Thyme out of Attica, but there is great difficult in raising it from seed." This was the experience of the Roman writer and naturalist who lived in the reigns of Nero and Vespasian. (The *Natural History* was published in 77 A.D., two years before Pliny's death in the volcanic eruption that demolished Pompeii.) His experience is repeated today by gardeners who try to grow all kinds of thyme from seed. The seeds of creeping thymes (*T. serpyllum* and varieties) germinate sparsely and the seedlings grow slowly. Because of this, seedsmen seldom collect the seeds. By comparison, the seeds of *T. vulgaris* germinate freely, though the plants are slow in developing.

If you wish to grow common thyme from seeds, level a bed of well-prepared, pulverized soil in the place where you want plants to mature. Make a wide bed, digging out all grass and weeds and cultivating to a depth of 6 inches in sandy soil, and to 12 inches in heavy, clayey soil. Broadcast the fine seeds thickly, cover with a sprinkling of soil, then dampen down with a misty spray. Seeds put in pockets among rocks will yield fragrant plants that nestle against the stones in a natural way.

Winter Care of Thymes

Thymes have a genius for survival, although good gardeners do not trade on this fact, but are simply grateful for it. I have found that plants which appear winter-killed often are only damaged back to main roots. For this reason, I do not trim them close in fall, but leave about 3 inches above ground and cover with salt hay for winter protection. If thymes grow near the house where the winter appearance is important, mulch with juniper boughs or pine. Be watchful of heaving when ground begins to thaw in late winter.

A thick planting of thyme always looks like a weeding problem, but usually mats can be lifted back with care for the main roots, which go down 12 inches or more, and roots of weeds and grass extracted with a dandelion digger. Clover is the worst invader of thyme; it must be dug out vigilantly before it becomes established. But there is no pleasanter gardening chore than removing weeds from a bed of thyme. A cloud of fragrance rises as you lift the heavy mats to extract the offending weeds. And what joy to stand back and view a mound of thyme cleared of every weed.

He who would know humility
Must weed a bed of thyme.
—A.G.S.

Thyme and Its Varieties

Whether you grow thymes for use in the kitchen, as ground covers or small hedges, or in a selected collection, you will find them a confusing family, with identification sometimes difficult, sometimes impossible. A named collection needs to be planted separate from one another; otherwise species and varieties grow from one bed to another, intermingling and cross-pollinating with the strong growers ousting the less vigorous.

In two or three years a hillside of the more rampant thymes becomes a rich tapestry of grays and greens, in bloom a rival to heather. Here it does not matter if different kinds intermingle somewhat, though the effect is better if they do not mix completely.

Creeping thyme is known as "mother of thyme."

There are two well-known species of thyme—*Thymus serpyllum,* the creeping thyme or "mother-of-thyme", and *Thymus vulgaris,* common or culinary thyme.

The *serpyllum* group is further divided into those of flat or creeping growth (not over 3 inches), and those that form mats (to 6 inches while in flower, with well-established plants growing even taller). Some are gold-leaved, some misty blue-green or gray-green, others between dark green and chartreuse. Spring-planted, these thymes will be ready to spread and cover by fall. The next year they will form walks or make lawns to replace grass, and they can be walked upon without harm.

The common thymes *(T. vulgaris)* are used for seasoning, traditionally a part of every culinary garden. However, they are so fragrant and attractive that many gardeners now plant them as shrubby hedges to border paths, outline beds, and assist in the tracing of patterns and designs in formal gardens. These hedges are low, not above 12 inches, and may be trimmed for conformity. Clippings can be dried for seasonings and potpourri, or to make thyme tea.

VI

May Day Party

Upon the first of May,
With garlands fresh and gay,
With mirth and music sweet,
For such a season meet,
They passe their time away
—OLD SONG

The May Day party at Caprilands is planned to bring us a little of the charm, wonder, and magic long associated with the advent of spring. We can't ride into the wood on caparisoned steeds or tramp the night through to the lights of Walpurgis Night; we no longer fertilize fields with ashes from fires that burned witches, nor do we drive cattle through flames to keep them safe for another year. Seldom do we go singing with arm-filling garlands or hang May baskets on doors, but at Caprilands we recall these customs as we celebrate the end of winter and salute the new gardening year with a May Day party.

Sweet Woodruff, May Day Symbol

We honor on this happy day a modest plant of the woods, called sweet woodruff, *Asperula odorata,* which carpets the forests in Germany with glossy leaves and tiny white blossoms. The green plant has a mossy smell, but let there be one dry leaf and you will sense all the

The punch bowl is a traditional part of the May Day party at Caprilands.

sweetness of May. This is due to the sweet principle of coumarin which has the fragrance of new-mown hay and is a fixative for other odors.

Sweet woodruff makes an excellent ground cover and, as such, is increasingly appreciated by gardeners and landscape architects. A shady site is best where soil is humusy, moist and acid. Gather woodruff for the rose jar and for making sachet; place sprigs in letters to your gardening friends.

From my youth I recall that elusive smell of woods in spring—a sweetness ascending from mold and decay but with the breath of young life rising from it. That is the odor of sweet woodruff.

May Day Traditions

To be traditional, food for May Day should come largely from the dairy. Eggs, milk, and oatmeal cakes were the ancient fare, prepared and served around the Beltane fires of Scotland and similar fires in other parts of Europe. The first day of May was called Beltane or Baltein, and the great event was the *tein-eigen* or "forced fire." This bonfire was of Druidic origin and flamed on the highest points of accessible land where dwelt the Druid gods.

Village fires were extinguished so that the hearths might be lighted later in the newness of spring with a faggot from the Beltane fire.

Recipes for a May Day Party

Spread with Sardines and Tarragon

- 8 ounces of cream cheese
- 2 ounces sardines, packed in water
- 2 capers
- ¼ teaspoon tarragon, dried
- 2 sprigs fresh tarragon
- 1 teaspoon chopped onion or chives

Blend cream cheese with all ingredients. Serve with crackers or toast points.

Makes about 1 cup.

Strawberry and Woodruff Tea

Take equal quantities of young strawberries and woodruff leaves. Pour 1 quart of boiling water over it, allow to set for 15 minutes. Strain and serve with honey as a sweetener.

Makes 4 cups.

Sorrel Soup

- 1 cup fresh French sorrel leaves
- 6 leeks or 4 shallots or 1 medium onion, chopped
- 1 clove garlic, crushed
- 3 tablespoons butter
- 6 cups chicken stock
- 4 potatoes, boiled, pared and cubed
- 1 sprig rosemary
- chopped parsley or chives for garnish

In a saucepan, saute sorrel, leeks, shallots or onion, and garlic in butter until soft, but not browned. Add stock. Cover, cook on medium heat for 30 minutes. Reduce heat to low. Stir in potatoes and rosemary. Reheat to simmering, but do not boil. Garnish with parsley or chives. Serve with garlic bread croutons.

Serves 6 to 8.

Spring Green Spread

Blend all ingredients, using enough milk or apple juice to make spreadable.
Makes about 1 cup.

- 3 ounces cream cheese
- 4 tablespoons finely chopped burnet leaves
- 2 tablespoons chopped chives
- ¼ cup chopped lettuce and parsley mixture
- 2 tablespoons milk or apple juice
- pepper, if desired

Sesame Cookies

Preheat oven to 400°. Toast sesame seeds in a large frying pan over low heat for about 5 minutes or until they are browned, being careful not to burn them. Stir frequently with a wooden spoon. (Sesame seeds are filled with oil, so no extra grease is needed.) Combine eggs, honey, butter and hot sesame seeds and beat until well blended. Sift together flour and baking powder, and add to sesame seed mixture. Beat well. Add extracts and beat again until batter is smooth. Grease cookie sheets with non-stick spray. Drop generous half teaspoons of dough onto cookie sheets about 2 inches apart. Bake at 400° until cookies are well browned on the edges, about 8 minutes. Use a spatula to move cookies to a wire rack. Cool. Store cookies in an airtight container. (Do not refrigerate.)
Makes 6 to 8 dozen.

- 1 cup sesame seeds
- 4 eggs, beaten
- 1 cup plus 1 tablespoon honey
- ¾ cup butter (1½ sticks), room temperature
- 1 cup unbleached white flour
- 1 cup whole wheat pastry flour
- 1 teaspoon baking powder
- 1 teaspoon vanilla extract
- 1 teaspoon almond extract

A Quick and Different Salad

Arrange oranges, onions, and tomatoes on lettuce. Blend the remaining ingredients and use as a dressing. Garnish the salad with flowers and fresh herbs.
Serves 6 to 8.

- 3 oranges, peeled and sliced
- 3 red Italian onions, sliced thin
- 3 tomatoes, sliced thin
- lettuce

- ½ cup honey
- ½ cup olive oil
- ½ cup basil vinegar
- 1 clove garlic, crushed
- ½ cup fresh basil (or 1 tablespoon dried)

- flowers and fresh herbs for garnish

A Morris dancer provides entertainment.

The heat and the flames of this great conflagration streaming up to heaven and exploding in bright showers of rapidly burning birch had properties of magic and healing. In the holocaust old man winter perished; indeed, he was often burned in effigy, a man of straw thrown into the flames after ritual songs and processions. As the straw body, cornhusks, and birch boughs were consumed, spectators reached into the fire to retrieve charred bits as good luck charms.

Around the flaming pyre the country people sat at a table made of green sod and large enough to accommodate them all. A cooking fire was kindled, a custard prepared, and a great thin oatmeal cake called a bannock was divided among the company. It was solemnly eaten for it marked an occasion compounded of wild joy and great awe when the evils of death, of which winter was symbolic, were driven out, and the resurrection of life occurred, symbolized by spring.

This merry month has been a time of worship as well as feasting since the dawn of history. Truly it is the flower month when Greeks and Romans worshipped Flora, Goddess of Flowers; now May is dedicated to the Virgin Mary. May is a time for rejoicing; the month for Maypole dances, May baskets, and May flowers.

Decorations for May Day

My decorations for May Day feature a high-pedestaled, milk-glass bowl with punch cups around it and a deep tray underneath with a little water in it to keep fresh the covering of lilac leaves. I surround the tray with bright herbal flowers from the garden, with basket-of-gold alyssum, myrtle, sweet violets, and Johnny-jump-ups—these interspersed with young camomile plants and crocuses. This garland keeps well and shows off the many cuttings of sweet woodruff which I insert in small containers of moist, mossy soil that are concealed by the other flowers and leaves.

Visitors to Caprilands on May Day frolic around the May Pole.

VII

The Herbal Salad

"In Health, if Sallet Herbs, you can't endure, Sick, you'll desire them, or for Food or Cure." We present you a taste of our English garden Housewifry in the matter of Sallets. And though some of them may be vulgar, as are most of the best things, yet we impart them to show the plenty, riches, and variety of the Sallet-Garden. And to justify what has been asserted of the possibility of living (not unhappily) on Herbs and Plants according to Divine institution.

—*JOHN EVELYN, ACETARIA,* 1699

The herbal salad is comprised of heads of lettuce, chicory, endive, and other garden greens when available. We shred or cut our greens until they are in fine form, for we serve about 75 people from our massive salad bowl, and find that the cut greens are easier to handle, both for us and for our guests than large pieces. After the bowl is filled, the decoration of the top begins with a trip through the garden to determine which flowers, vegetables and herbs are appropriate for the theme of the day.

Here are some of the colorful items that make the design for the top of the bowl:

In the Spring, there are chives, chive blossoms, Egyptian onion stalks, sweet cicely leaves and blossoms, parsley, violets and violet leaves, sometimes camomile (we use both the flowers and the delicate apple-scented foliage.) Mint leaves at this time are tender and green, or darkly purple, like the orange mint. Nepeta blossoms are brightly

Recipes for Salads and Flowers

Fennel Salad

- 1 large bunch fennel
- 2 onions, chopped
- 2 cups tomatoes, chopped
- ¼ cup pine nuts
- ½ cup raisins
- 4 cups spinach, torn in pieces

- ½ cup olive oil
- 6 ounces sardines, packed in water, chopped
- 1 tablespoon fennel seed
- ½ cup tarragon vinegar
- 2 cloves garlic, crushed
- 1 teaspoon mixed herbs

Cut the fennel into very small pieces and put in a wooden bowl well-rubbed with garlic. Add chopped onions, tomatoes, pine nuts, raisins, and spinach.

In a separate bowl prepare the dressing by mixing well the olive oil, sardines, fennel seed, vinegar, crushed garlic, and herbs.

Dress the fennel salad, tossing the greens to incorporate all the mixture.

Serves 6 *to* 8.

Fennel and Escarole Salad

- 1 head escarole, cut into small pieces
- 1 large bunch fennel, cut finely to make 4 cups
- 6 stalks celery, finely chopped
- 2 green peppers, sliced
- 12 artichokes
- 4 hard-cooked eggs, cut in quarters
- 1 cooked Italian sausage, sliced
- 6 slices Italian mozzarella cheese, cut into strips
- 1 cup onions, chopped (scallions or Egyptian)

Toss the above ingredients together and dress with a French dressing.

Serves 6 *to* 8.

Strange Salad but Good

- oranges, grapes, and bananas, sliced
- watercress or upland cress
- green onions, scallions, or Egyptian onions, chopped

Arrange the fruit slices attractively on the cress. Add chopped onions. Dress with a sharp French dressing containing tarragon.

Marigold Biscuits

Add the calendula flowers and parsley to the biscuit dough and bake as usual.
Makes 2 dozen.

- 1 cup fresh calendula flowers (pot marigold), or ½ cup dried
- ¼ cup chopped parsley
- 1 recipe baking powder biscuit dough

A Grand Sallet of Divers Compounds

Take green purslane and pick it leaf by leaf and wash it and swing it in a napkin. Then being dished in a faire, clean dish and finely piled up in a heap in the midst of it, lay round about the center of the sallet, pickled capers, currants and raisins of the sun, washed, picked, mingled and laid round about it; about them some carved cucumbers, in slices or halves, and laid round also. Then garnish the dish brims with borage, or clove gillyflowers, or other ways with cucumber peels, olives, capers, and raisins of the sun, then the best Sallet oyl and wine vinegar.

From John Evelyn

Marigold Soup

Combine chicken stock, rice, celery, onions, potatoes and crushed pepper in a large saucepan. Bring to a boil, reduce heat, and simmer, covered for 20 minutes, or until rice is just cooked. Add spinach, chives, parsley, calendula flowers and leaves and cook 5 minutes more. Remove from heat and stir in lemon juice. Garnish with fresh calendula heads. Serve at once with a flower in each bowl.
Serves 10 to 12.

- 8 cups chicken stock
- ½ cup brown rice, uncooked
- 1 cup chopped celery
- 2 medium onions, chopped
- 2 medium potatoes, scrubbed and diced
- 1 tablespoon black peppercorns, crushed
- 2 cups fresh spinach, chopped
- 1 cup chopped chives
- 1 cup parsley, chopped
- 2 cups calendula flowers (pot marigold)
- 1 cup young calendula leaves (pot marigold)
- 1 tablespoon lemon juice (or more, to taste)
- calendula flower heads for garnish

Chive blossoms can be used to add color to an herbal salad.

blue, and, while not of very good taste, are pretty in the landscape picture that will evolve from this collection. We never can resist having a few daffodils (though we do not eat them) tucked into the end of the design; they are so much a part of the season. Grated carrots always form a part of the pattern and are used all through the year. Apple blossoms are not to be forgotten, and our numerous viburnums start to produce their fragrant flowers toward the end of May and are incorporated in some of the designs. Even a Ballerina Poppy may find itself in a late spring picture.

The Salad, Complete with Flowers

Thirty years ago when Caprilands started its herbal luncheons and invited guests who were interested in gardening and garden cookery for the lecture and luncheon, we used many flowers in foods, both for flavor and appearance. Our guests, unused to this vernal decoration, were hesitant to try many of our efforts, and were astonished indeed to see a salad topped with nasturtiums and calendulas, or cookies with real rose buds pressed into the frosted tops, and punch bowls on which floated violets, carnations (pinks), and Johnny jumpups (viola tricolor). It took some persuasion and the telling of many tall stories to overcome this fear of "eating the daisies," but I was a firm believer in beautifying foods and in using the things that are at hand, so continued to do so. We candied violets, roses and mint leaves for condiments and did decorations in the time-honored way, but when we were pressed for time, we used the natural untreated flower and many times found it more acceptable and effective, certainly less time consuming.

Johnny jumpups may be used as floating decorations on a bowl of punch.

In the years that have followed, for our increased numbers of luncheon programs and many new guests we have continued to use our own style of floral foods, some invented, and some garnered from other sources. Today there is less astonishment and more appreciation. Books and magazine articles have revived recipes long forgotten and have proved that we were then more daring than original. Flowers and herbs decorate the places set on our tables, a fragrant note usually liked by even the most prosaic and literal minded. They are conversation pieces which often start discussions.

At the present time we have a number of kitchen artists who do such fascinating floral and vegetable landscapes with our salad bowl that we are reluctant to toss and serve them, thus disturbing the picture. We, of course, do not use anything that is not edible, although some of the flowers have little taste and these we remove as we mix the greens. Cameras click as we show the colorful bowl (carried by one of our girls, bending under its weight, to all three of our serving rooms), but few pictures show it as it really is, and none can give you an idea of its delicious smell.

Summer

The Caprilands dooryard garden bids visitors welcome.

On a stroll through the gardens Adelma Simmons finds plants that need attention.

Herb gardens provide a background for rest and contemplation.

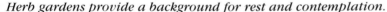

A fresh full cabbage can look as beautiful as a rose.

Ham and pea salad is flavored with mint.

A brick pathway provides a cozy place for a cat to stretch.

Silver and gray-green leaves suggest coolness on a hot summer day.

Celosia blooms in several shades and is a useful everlasting.

VIII

Summer Diary

To have nothing here but Sweet Herbs, and those only choice ones too, and every kind its bed by itself.

—*ERASMUS*

Summer in the herb garden is a time of rare delight when days are long but never long enough, when the plans of winter are realized and the labors of spring come to fruition, and harvesting begins in earnest. Come with me in the early hours of day for a walk through the garden.

The folded leaves of Lady's mantle, *Alchemilla,* are then filled with dewdrops like gems, reminding us that dawn was the hour when dew had magic powers. The plant was thought to impact great virtues to the dew drops that settled on each leaf with its look of a pleated mantle, fresh and lovely enough for the Holy Lady. I have alchemilla planted at the head of a cross of thyme in the Saints Garden where the yellow fragrant flowers rise like a morning offering of pale gold to the Virgin and Child above.

At one corner of the weathered fence, tall teasels holding water in the leaf axils tempt me to try an ancient early-morning beauty treatment—"Who washes her face in this precious water removes all blemishes." Teasel, once called "Venus' basin," was later Christianized to "Our Lady's basin." Hummingbirds drink of this water, and many insects are tempted by it. Later they will have eaten out the leaf lining so that the teasel basins no longer hold water.

At the foot of the statue of St. Fiacre a mass of calendulas, "Mary's gold," reaches toward the sun. "Only to look on marigold will draw evil humors out of the head and strengthen the eysight," so ran the old saying. In the Middle Ages the flowers were used to decorate the rich robes of church statues and in the monastery gardens of southern Europe, calendulas blossomed for every festival of Mary.

Oddly enough, the marigold was not named for the Virgin; this association came later in medieval times. Rather the name was a corruption of the Anglo-Saxon *mersomeargealla,* "the marsh marigold," which is, of course, *Caltha* not *Calendula.* In old English the name was "goldes" or "ruddes," and more recently the marigold. In an herbal dawn we think, too, of Shakespeare's Friar Lawrence who collected baskets of potent herbs for Juliet's sleep.

To look on "goldes" always strengthens me for the day's work as I go up the hill for coffee in the dooryard garden. This is one of summer's special pleasures to be enjoyed from the comfort of a well-cushioned, weather-beaten chair before the day's problems must be confronted.

The dooryard garden at this hour is bursting with sweetness. There are peppermint, apple, and rose geraniums, rosemarys, thymes, lavenders, and a great terracotta tub overflowing with a tall lemon geranium. Still other plants beside the door are convenient for picking as we prepare a meal. After coffee, we pause to admire the mints for they belong particularly to summer mornings. The little path leading to the greenhouse spills over with orange mint and frequently is even choked with curly mint. These will soon be harvested, however, for I cut them often, using fresh green leaves for jelly and drying an abundance in onion baskets over the kitchen stove for later enjoyment in teas and potpourri.

Shades of gold include calendulas and marigolds.

IX

Summer Garden Care

The good care you give your herb garden in summer is the key to its prosperity at other seasons. Now is the time to renew the excitement you felt last winter when the garden was only a dream sketched on a piece of graph paper, and to summon up the fine optimism of spring when it was so wonderful to be outdoors again. Certainly you need enthusiasm now for the many chores of maintenance. It takes work to keep an herb garden healthy for a good harvest. The routine is like a three-act play, with Act I setting the scene (watering, mulching, and feeding); Act II producing the villains (weeds, insects, and disease); Act III ending happily with the harvest, the sowing of seeds for early fall crops, and surely, time, too, to gaze upon the garden with pleasure.

Mulching the Herb Garden

After your planting is done, weed the garden clean. Then mulch every bit of bare ground to a depth of 2 inches with buckwheat or cocoa hulls, or other mulching material available in your area. Mix a little sand or soil with these light mulches or wet them down thoroughly for they have a tendency to blow away. As holes appear in the mulch, replenish it. Some mulches like peat moss and half-decayed leaves work into the soil each winter and need to be renewed in spring. Others like buckwheat and cocoa hulls stay pretty much in place.

A mulch laid in spring after weeding serves several good purposes: it conserves moisture, it helps keep down new weeds, and it gives the garden a neat, well-cared-for appearance.

Avoid acid mulches like pine needles or sphagnum peat moss for shade-loving plants—most herbs like sweet soil. Our choice is cocoa hulls.

Feeding Herbs

Herbs grown in well-drained soil with plenty of sun and warmth will do reasonably well, but they will really flourish if given fertilizer. Quick-growing annuals like dill and borage benefit from a generous amount of well-rotted manure (or the dried commercial product) worked into the soil before planting. Lime is an essential for most herbs.

It is true that over-fertilized herbs are not as good for seasonings; on the other hand, an impoverished soil produces stunted plants and poor leaves for cutting. I find it best to enrich the herb garden scantily with well-rotted manure or compost in spring. Then I water during the season with liquid manure or "tea" made of rich compost.

Potted herbs, such as lemon verbenas in large tubs and window boxes of geraniums, need regular feeding through the growing season with a liquid houseplant fertilizer, applied as a thorough watering once every two or three weeks. Plants in containers have little space in which to send roots out in search of food, and in mid-summer the soil dries out rapidly requiring such frequent watering that nutrients leach out quickly. Often a potted herb that looks less healthy than usual will quickly regain good color if given liquid fertilizer.

Pause to Appreciate Your Garden

It is in summer that we need time to enjoy our gardens. In the cool of early morning evaluate your plants and appreciate their beauty. Brush fragrant plants, roll a leaf or two in your hand, and breathe in the wonderful aroma. This is a good hour, too, to view your garden objectively; to see if leaf textures, colors, and contrasts are pleasing; whether one clump is too large, another needs moving toward the back of the border, and a third would look better in other company. Make notes of your decisions and pin them to your bulletin board or clip to your desk pad, so that when fall and spring planting times come you can easily make improvements.

In the evening, as the sun goes down, make another tour of your garden. Maybe pull a few weeds always visible at this hour of the day. Then walk in the dusk of evening, forget the weeds, the plans and the problems, and enjoy the tall spires of the artemisias; stay out until the moon touches all with quiet beauty.

Summer garden care includes routine weeding.

Mulching conserves moisture, keeps down weeds, and makes a garden look neat.

Watering with compost tea is a good way to enrich the herb garden during the summer.

Early summer mornings are a good time to view the garden objectively; here Adelma Simmons does just that.

X

Mints and Midsummer

Come buy my mint, my fine green mint!
Let none despise the merry, merry cries
of famous London town.
—*OLD LONDON STREET CRY*

There are few plants in the garden as loved and useful, or as despised for their rankness, as the mints. To know them is to love them—and to be wary also of their bold entrances into every domain of the garden. They are no respecters of the rights of neighboring plants. They run through walks, cover the cowering plants that cannot avoid their advances and often destroy the gardener's dream of order and neatness.

It would be hard to face a springtime garden without the curls of mint pushing through the brown soil. While they are not the first herbs to appear, few plants are as fresh or as perfect upon emerging from the earth. They look like hundreds of small green roses opening to the world of spring, and touching stirs up rich odors.

Some Ways to Enjoy Mints

I border grassy paths with various mints, where the lawn mower keeps them cut and they may run at will. As we walk through the garden we can smell the cool odor of mint everywhere. No matter how much you enjoy mint at other times of the year, it is indisputably a plant for tasting and smelling in hot summer weather.

In ancient Greece and Rome, mint was a scent used by rich and poor, and it was the custom to rub tables with it before guests were seated. Today orange mint has many uses in the modern home. To scent a room, hang bunches of mint from open doors or archways where a breeze will release the aroma. This is a practice in India, and I am told that in many hot countries large bunches of mint are tied to screen doors to send cool odors through the house.

On hot summer days when even the coolest garden flowers appear wilted, put bowls of mint on your tables. They will look and smell cool. When you are entertaining, place a spring of mint on each napkin at the table. On hot summer days we use mint leaves, especially curly and apple mint, or lemon verbena in pitchers of ice water.

In this day of dining and entertaining out of doors, mints make fine terrace or patio plants. They thrive in redwood tubs, in large clay or pottery containers, or in plant pockets in terrace pavements. In using mints this way, be sure to provide drainage and evenly moist soil. Clip them back occasionally for a neat appearance.

To know mint is to love it.

Mint can be used as an edible decoration on many kinds of food. Pineapple mint adds a lovely fragrance to the table as it decorates the napkins in this table setting.

The Fascinating History of Mint

Herbals are filled with references to the virtues of mint. Chaucer speaks of, "A little path of mintes full and fenill green," and Gerard tells us: "The smelle rejoiceth the heart of man, for which cause they used to strew it in chambers of places of recreation, pleasure and repose where feasts and banquets are made. . . . It is applied with salt to bitings of mad dogs. They lay it on the stinging of wasps with good success. The smell of minte does stir up the minde and the taste to a greedy desire of meate."

Parkinson wrote, "Mintes are sometimes used in baths with balm and other herbs as a help to comfort and strengthen the nerves and sinews. It is much used either outwardly applied or inwardly drunk to strengthen and comfort weak stomackes."

Culpeper describes cures affected with mint: "Rose leaves and mint, heated and applied outwardly, cause rest and sleep. . . . The leaves of wild or horsemint, such as grows in ditches, are serviceable to dissolve wind in the stomach, to help the colic and those that are short-winded, and they are an especial remedy for those who have veneral dreams in the night. The juice dropped in the ears eases the pains of them and destroys the worms that breed therein . . . [the leaves] are extremely bad for wounded people; and they say a wounded man who eats mint, his wound will never be cured, and that is a long day."

Mint is Biblical and is thought to have originated in Mediterranean lands. Some varieties, slight variations of *Mentha spicata,* came from Egypt and the Holy Land. Mint was brought from the East in commerce and probably was carried by the crusaders into northern and central Europe. In all these places it thrived and, as in our gardens, took over, finding the sites it liked best, usually near water. There it grew luxuriously and was usually considered a native plant.

Mint was once a Biblical tithe. In Matthew 23:23 we read, "Woe unto you, scribes and Pharisees, hypocrites! for ye pay tithe of mint, and anise, and cummin, and have omitted the weightier matters of the law, judgment, mercy, and faith: these ought ye to have done, not to leave the other undone." Peoples of the East and Near East including southern Europeans, Greeks, and Romans used mint as a condiment, in salads, and for flavoring and medicine far more than we do.

Mints have been known as "strewing herbs" since men first thought of such refinements. It was noted that breathing the essence of mint cleared the head and aroused the senses. It also destroyed unpleasant odors when it was scattered over the floors of synagogues, temples, and churches. In medieval Europe, mints with thyme, rosemary, and pennyroyal were scattered among the rushes that covered the stone floors of castles and the earthen floors of cottages. Here they purified the air with fragrance that rose up with every step.

The generic name *Mentha,* was applied first by Theophrastus, a Greek philospher-scientist and herbalist who succeeded Aristotle as head of the lyceum in 322 B.C. In mythology Mintho was a nymph of great beauty who was loved by Pluto, god of the underworld. Persephone became jealous of Pluto's attachment and changed the nymph into the fragrant but lowly mint. Since that day mints have been grown in the shady areas of the dark world of Pluto.

Some Useful Mints

Bergamot or orange mint *(M. citrata)* is a treasure, for it is the most fragrant and manageable of all the species that I grow. The dark green leaves are rounded, broad, and touched with purple. Sometimes the undersides take on a deep shade of red; in early spring the whole plant is distinctly reddish purple. As the season advances, leaves become green and are ripe for cutting. I cut orange mint many times during the summer and use it in the making of a very special punch.

Orange mint appears in many of my summer flower arrangements and frequently surrounds my punch bowl. There, tucked into moist sphagnum moss, it takes root and continues to grow. I harvest the leaves and tender stems two or three times and dry them for winter teas.

Pennyroyal *(M. pulegium),* a charming creeper, a dense aromatic mat of glossy leaves, travels fast and makes an excellent ground cover but unfortunately is not winter-hardy. Sometimes I winter plants close to the greenhouse under cover, but seldom do they live through sub-zero weather. Therefore, to be sure I have some another year, I always take a few plants inside. In a home greenhouse this mint will trail over the edge of a bench and smell sweet as you brush by it. It is lovely in a hanging basket. Pennyroyal has long been used for tea, and was a favorite flavoring for puddings in the days when ground meat was termed a "pudding." It is, however, toxic and dangerous to use in any large amount. An infusion of the leaves has been used by herbalists for spasms, cramps, and colds, but it must be taken with the greatest discretion.

Doubtless the best known use of pennyroyal is its effectiveness in warding off insects, particularly fleas. In fact, one of its old names was "flea-away." The oil of pennyroyal was spread in pantries to keep away ants and other pests. Some people rub their pets with it, and some rub themselves with it to keep mosquitoes away. The Greeks used pennyroyal as a seasoning for meat and it was called *blekon* or *glekon.* It had many familiar names in England, such as "lurk-in-the-ditch" and "run-by-the-ground." In the days when people wore wreaths to impart virtues to the brain, pennyroyal offered a popular and pleasant way to clear the mental processes.

Recipes with Mint

Mint Salad Plate

- pear and apple slices
- mint leaves
- caraway seeds
- toasted almonds

- ½ cup salad oil
- 1 cup orange mint, finely chopped
- 1 lemon, juice of
- 1 orange, juice of
- 2 tablespoons mint vinegar
- 2 tablespoons honey (optional)

Arrange the fruit slices on a bed of mint leaves. Sprinkle with caraway seeds and toasted almonds. Mix the remaining ingredients to make a dressing, and pour over. Hint: For a special flavor, allow the mint to stand in the oil overnight.

Pork and Pea Salad with Mint Dressing

- 2 cups frozen peas, steamed
- 1 cup cubed cooked pork
- ½ cup chopped onion
- ¼ cup chopped leeks
- 4 stalks chopped celery
- ¼ cup chopped parsley
- 2 potatoes, cooked and cubed
- ½ cup mint leaves, chopped

- ½ cup olive oil
- ¼ cup mint vinegar
- black pepper
- ½ cup mint leaves

In a large bowl combine peas, pork, onion, leeks, celery, parsley, potatoes and mint leaves. Whisk olive oil, mint vinegar, black pepper and mint leaves together. Pour dressing over meat and vegetable mixture. Combine well.
Serves 8.

Orange Mint Punch

- 1 cup mint leaves (preferably orange mint)
- 2 tablespoons honey
- 2 cups water
- 6 decaffeinated tea bags
- 12 cups boiling water
- 12 ounces frozen orange juice

Mix mint, honey and two cups water in a large saucepan. Simmer over low heat for 10 minutes. Remove from heat. Add tea bags and boiling water to mint mixture. Allow to cool for about ½ hour. Remove tea bags, then add orange juice and mix well. Refrigerate until cold. To serve, pour orange tea over a chunk of ice in a punch bowl.
Makes about 15 cups.

A Luncheon Salad

In a large bowl toss lettuce, carrots, peas, and mint together. Whisk oil, vinegar and nuts together. Pour dressing over salad and toss. Serve immediately.

Serves 4 to 6.

- 1 head lettuce, broken into bite-size pieces
- ½ cup shredded carrots
- ½ cup peas, cooked
- ½ cup mint, chopped (spearmint, curly or apple)

- ½ cup olive oil
- ¼ cup mint vinegar
- ¼ cup almonds or walnuts, chopped

Carrot and Orange Soup

Melt butter in a large saucepan. Add onions and saute over medium heat until soft. Add carrots, chicken broth, pepper and ground cloves. Cover and simmer over medium heat until carrots are tender, about 15 minutes. Remove about ¼ cup of soup stock. Mix flour with stock and return it to the pan. Cook, stirring, about 5 minutes longer. Remove pan from heat and cool 15–20 minutes. Stir garlic, shallots and mint into cooled soup.

Puree the soup in batches in a food processor or blender until smooth. Pour pureed soup into a serving bowl, stir in lemon and orange juices, cover and chill thoroughly. Serve soup in chilled bowls, garnished with orange slices or mint.

Serves 12 (8 cups).

- 2 tablespoons butter
- 2 medium onions, chopped
- 8 large carrots, scrubbed and sliced (about 5 cups)
- 3 cups chicken broth
- ¼ teaspoon white pepper
- ¼ teaspoon ground cloves
- 2 tablespoons flour
- 1 clove garlic, chopped
- 1 teaspoon chopped shallots
- ½ cup fresh mint leaves, loosely packed
- juice of ½ lemon
- 2 cups orange juice

Caprilands Pea Soup

Place peas and potatoes in saucepan with 2 quarts water. Add onions and garlic and cook together until mixture becomes a thick mush. Add peppercorns, mint, thyme, bay leaf, chicken broth and water. Let simmer for ½ hour.

Cool slightly and blend in batches in a blender or food processor. Return to pot. Add 1 can evaporated milk (2 cans if you wish to extend soup and make it a cream type). Sprinkle with paprika and mint leaves.

Serves 12.

- 1 pound split green peas
- 4 medium potatoes, peeled
- 2 quarts water
- 2 onions, sliced
- 2 cloves garlic, mashed
- 6 peppercorns, crushed
- 4 sprigs mint
- 1 teaspoon dried thyme
- 1 bay leaf
- 2 teaspoons Barth's instant chicken broth
- 2 cups water
- 1 or 2 cans evaporated milk
- paprika and mint leaves for garnish

Wild American pennyroyal is very strong-smelling. We border our culinary herbs with it as a protective measure against pests.

The apple mint *(M. suaveolens)* often starts in the herb garden as a small plant, but it usually ends up growing around the compost pile, in the dump, or perhaps it will jump a fence and grow happily in the pasture or in a neighbor's yard. It was once used in the monasteries of Europe for the treatment of epilepsy. The monks found it valuable in relieving the languor following an attack. Today it still grows around the ruins of ancient buildings, a fragrant reminder of those first centers for the treatment of the sick. I enjoy this mint around an old foundation that needs some cover. It grows either in sun or shade, rich or lean soil, and the soft gray-green fuzzy leaves, and tall growth make it an attractive cover for an unsightly spot. Blossoms are gray-white, shading to pink or pale purple. I make at least three cuttings of it each year and start drying for winter teas in June, continuing the harvest until October. From frequent cutting the leaves are more tender and better for making the candied mint leaves I use to decorate cakes.

The pineapple mint *(M. suaveolens* var. *variegata)* is a small form (to 18 inches) of the apple mint with white-splotched leaves that vary with the seasons. I find it needs some winter protection although I wintered it outdoors without trouble for many years. In a cool spot in the house the plant will be attractive from autumn to spring in a hanging basket or trailing from a window box. I use leaves of this and pineapple sage to decorate jellied fruit desserts or fruit cups. While it has little taste, the odor is wonderful.

Mint was once a Biblical tithe.

Growing and Propagating the Mints

Actually mints will grow almost anywhere. They thrive in moist, humusy soil in shade but also in sun, and few pests ever bother them. The only problem with mints is that they spread too rapidly, overrunning other plants and growing into a mass instead of staying in neat separate clumps. To avoid this, it is suggested you can plant each clump of mint in a metal barrel, with top and bottom removed and sunk 18 inches into the ground. Or insert metal strips 12 to 18 inches deep around the plantings of mint.

I have never curbed mint this way, but from long experience, I check on the growth of the runners twice a year, transplanting from the garden any that seem out of place, or cutting runners with a sharp tool. I keep mints well in bounds in the Butterfly Garden where they occupy one bed by themselves. During the growing season I use the plants lavishly. They are cut in summer to make jellies, vinegars, and an essence for lamb sauce. Leaves are candied and also dried for teas. They are fashioned in cooling bouquets for hot weather. If you use your mint beds in this way I am sure they will never be too large; more likely, they will not be large enough.

XI

Midsummer Party

Then doth the joyful feast of John
The Baptist take his turne,
When bonfires great, with lofty flame,
In everie towne doth burne;
And young men round about with maides
Do dance in everie street
With garlands wrought of Motherwort
Or else with Vervaine sweet.
—*ANONYMOUS*

The folklore of herbs takes us down many delightful paths. Here at the farm we hold pleasant little celebrations on days that in the past were of significance to gardening and farming people. We meet in the garden to discuss the legends, the plants, and the personages of the day or the season. We eat the foods that once had special meaning (though often in a modern form) and drink the beverages—or their equivalents. These celebrations are usually on the saints' days since whatever their origin, a saint's name has been given them with the passing years. Many of the foods and customs go back before recorded history, where truth, legend, and magic merge.

We have a celebration for midsummer, usually the twenty-second and twenty-third days of June, the time of the summer solstice, the longest days of the year. After this, days are shorter as the sun retraces its steps and drops toward the harvest season.

In the past, as long days gave way to earlier darkness, fear attacked ancient people, fear that the light would go forever, so fires were built on midsummer's eve throughout Western Europe. These fires were to hold warmth in the heavens, to keep the sun from losing its heat, to insure good growth of grain and flax, and health for cattle. Like the fires preceding May Day, they were kindled to burn witches and other dispensers of evil.

As Europe was Christianized, the summer solstice and St. John the Baptist's Day sometimes coincided with the twenty-third and became the Eve of St. John, and the fires became St. John's Fires. In sixteenth-century Germany, almost every village had its bonfire on the Eve of St. John. Men, women, and children gathered around to dance and sing, pray, and repeat charms. The herbs, mugwort or St. John's herb and vervain, were made into chaplets to wear for the ceremonies.

Mugwort wreaths were often worn and bunches of larkspur were held up to the flames. If the fire was gazed upon through the larkspur, eyesight would be keen for the rest of the year. As fires died down, herbs were thrown on the embers with the wish, "May ill luck depart, burnt up with these."

Capriland garden paths provide delightful surprises.

Wheels to represent the sun were wrapped with straw and smeared with pitch, lighted and rolled down hill toward water, this to insure good crops for the year. Cattle were driven through the fire to protect them from sickness and bewitching. Young couples jumped over the flames; the higher they leaped, the taller their crops would grow. Charred bits from the fires were preserved in the fields; a burned broom upright in the field insured the flax harvest; fire-blackened sticks were crossed at the entrance to a grain field; a charred wreath was treasured above a peasant girl's couch.

A piece of this wreath might serve to propitiate the thunder, or cure sick cattle, or cleanse the house from pestilence. Great were the blessings of the midsummer fires. In Sweden, Balder's Balefires are still a joyous occasion. Then the air is filled with witches flying to the Great Witch who dwells in the mountains; caves open, rocks split apart, and spirits come forth to dance until the rising flames drive them back into hiding.

As we make our herb chaplets of mugwort and vervain and give them their fiery baptism, we too wish for the old magic, "May ill luck depart, burnt up with these."

In Midsummer mullein blooms near a garden birdhouse.

Garden statues and the herbs themselves bring to mind legends and customs of ages past.

Recipes for a Midsummer Party

June Punch Bowl

- 1 cup rosemary leaves
- 3 stalks borage, stem, leaves and blossoms
- 1 gallon grape or apple juice or mixture
- 3 limes, juice of
- ½ cup honey
- ½ cup brown sugar
- 1 lime, sliced for garnish
- borage leaves and blossoms for garnish

Steep rosemary and borage in juices, honey and sugar in large jug, 3 hours at room temperature, or preferably 24 hours or longer in the refrigerator. At serving time, pour juice mixture over block of ice in punch bowl. Decorate with lime slices, fresh blossoms, and leaves. Hint: In late summer, we heap the cake of ice with peach slices and ladle a slice into each cup.
Makes 1 gallon.

Summer Squash Soup

- 3 medium summer squash (yellow squash preferrably)
- 4 cups chicken stock
- 1 cup chopped celery
- 3 medium onions, thinly sliced (about 2½ cups)
- 1 clove garlic, crushed
- 1 sprig fresh rosemary, minced
- 1 sprig fresh thyme, minced
- ½ cup chopped parsley (loosely packed)

Wash, trim, and slice squash. Steam the squash until it is tender. Puree the cooked squash in a blender or food processor and set it aside (about 1½ cups puree). Bring the chicken stock to a boil in a large saucepan. Add celery, onions, garlic, rosemary and thyme and simmer, covered, about 10 minutes or until vegetables are tender. Reduce heat to low, add reserved squash puree and parsley. Cook to heat through.
Yields 7 cups.

Salmon Puff

- 4 eggs
- 2 cups milk
- 1 cup finely ground unsalted soda crackers or matzoh
- 16 ounces canned red salmon
- ¼ cup parsley
- ¼ teaspoon dried tarragon
- ¼ teaspoon ground thyme

Preheat oven to 350°. In a medium bowl, beat eggs until light. Mix in milk and cracker crumbs. Drain salmon, discard dark skin and bones. Crumble remaining salmon into egg mixture. Add parsley, tarragon and thyme, and mix well. Pour mixture into a greased, shallow 1½- or 2-quart baking dish and bake at 350° for about 40 minutes or until cooked through.
Serves 6 to 8.

Cucumber Salad

Sprinkle cucumber slices with lemon juice and let stand in refrigerator for 3 hours, then drain. Mix with the sour cream and lemon juice and sprinkle with salad burnet.

Combine lemon rind, caviar, onion, and black pepper to taste to make dressing. Pour over and sprinkle salad with chopped parsley.

- 4 cucumbers, peeled and sliced thinly
- 1 tablespoon lemon juice
- 1 cup sour cream
- ½ lemon, juice of
- burnet, chopped

- lemon rind, grated from 1 lemon
- 2 tablespoons caviar
- 1 tablespoon minced onion
- black pepper
- chopped parsley

Viennese Salad

Combine cucumbers, lettuce, celery, eggs, parsley, and chives. Toss together. Boil potato slices until tender (Try some caraway seeds in the water for more flavor and light fluffy potatoes). Drain and set aside. Whisk together oil, vinegar, tarragon, and pepper to taste. Pour dressing over potatoes while they are still warm. Combine potatoes and dressing with cucumber mixture. Serve at once.

Serves 8.

- 2 cups sliced cucumbers
- 2 heads lettuce, finely chopped
- 2 cups celery, finely sliced
- 4 hard-cooked eggs, sliced
- 1 cup chopped parsley
- ½ cup chopped chives
- 6 potatoes, peeled and sliced

- ¾ cup olive oil
- ½ cup tarragon vinegar
- ¼ cup chopped fresh tarragon
- black pepper

Our Favorite Summer Salad

Cover a large platter with basil leaves. Arrange slices of tomatoes and onions so that they overlap. Spread the chopped onions and chives on top.

Add the herbs to the honey until it is thick with herbs. Mix with vinegar to make a dressing to pour over. Garnish with sprigs of basil and green onions. Hint: This salad is best when the tomatoes are really ripe and the basil leaves are crisp and prolific—late July and August at Caprilands.

- large basil leaves
- ripe tomatoes, sliced
- red Italian onions, sliced
- green onions, chopped
- chives, chopped

- 1 cup honey
- parsley, rosemary, chives, thyme basil
- 4 cloves garlic, crushed
- ½ cup basil vinegar
- sprigs of basil and green onions for garnish

Chicken and Tarragon Salad

- 2 cups diced cold chicken
- ½ cup tarragon vinegar
- 1 tablespoon capers
- 2 teaspoons prepared herb mustard
- 1 small onion, chopped
- black pepper to taste
- 1 cup mayonnaise
- ¼ cup yogurt
- mixed greens
- 4 hard-cooked eggs for garnish

Place chicken in medium bowl. Whisk together tarragon vinegar, capers, mustard, and onion. Pour over chicken. Sprinkle with pepper. Let stand one-half hour. Whisk together mayonnaise and yogurt. Combine with chicken and marinade. Line a plate or bowl with greens. Mound the chicken mixture in the center, draining off excessive marinade as you transfer it. Peel and quarter eggs and use for garnish.

Serves 8.

Green Sauce for Meat

- ½ cup olive oil
- ¼ cup lemon juice
- ½ cup finely chopped parsley
- ¼ cup chopped chives
- 1 shallot, chopped
- ½ cup chopped sorrel leaves
- 6 borage leaves, chopped
- 1 teaspoon capers, minced
- 2 stalks celery and leaves, chopped
- 2 hard-cooked eggs, minced.
- black papper, freshly ground

Blend together well olive oil and lemon juice. Add remaining ingredients. Blend and season with freshly ground black pepper to taste. Hint: Good with potatoes, too, barbecued dishes and cold meats.

Makes 3 cups.

Rose Cookies

- 1 cup butter
- ½ cup honey
- 2 eggs, beaten
- 1¼ cups unbleached flour
- 1½ cups whole wheat flour
- 1 teaspoon baking soda
- ½ teaspoon cream of tartar
- 2 tablespoons rose water or 1 teaspoon rose syrup
- 2 tablespoons caraway seeds
- raisins for garnish

Preheat oven to 375°. Cream together butter and honey. Add eggs and beat well. Sift flours with baking soda and cream of tartar. Add to creamed mixture. Stir in rose water or rose syrup and caraway seeds. Drop mixture by teaspoonfuls onto greased cookie sheets. Flatten slightly with moistened fingers and put a raisin in the center of each cookie. Bake in a 375° oven until lightly browned about 8–10 minutes. Remove from cookie sheets and cool on a wire rack.

Makes about 8 dozen.

XII

Special Summer Pleasures

The Piper's Silver Garden

This garden, though small, gives special pleasure in the summer. Walks of crushed stone give easy access to the raised curved beds. This makes a natural frame and is very photogenic. The beds look like draperies when translated to paper. They were never accurately measured but instead of being planned to the inch were scratched on a prepared surface with a tobacco hoe, my favorite tool. As I finished the sketch on the surface of the ground my gardeners followed me with brick for facing the beds, which are raised about six inches from the walks. We only measured by eye, but what the plan lacked in perfect symmetry the growth of the plants eventually covered.

The center bed is a clover leaf planted with lamb's-ears *(Stachys byzantina)* surrounded with small clipped santolinas. For the focal point we were delighted to find our leading Piping Boy, the center of our planting. He is often called the young god Pan although he is far more innocent looking and less elfin than the original. The lead of the figure is just the right color note for silver foliage, and he makes a graceful figure in the center of the clover leaf, contrasting with its snowy santolinas.

Does a silver garden sound monotonous—garish in sun, or dull and dreary on a rainy, chilly spring or fall day? We have sometimes heard this criticism but it is one with which we disagree. We have found it fascinating to watch our silver garden develop through the seasons and the years, cool and chaste in early morning; standing unwilted, soaking up the sun and heat in hot July and August; shimmering in the dawn; mysterious by moonlight. At the year's end it seems to welcome the first snow and lies happily buried in white drifts all winter.

To combat monotony, there are so many variants of silver plants in gray, gray-blue, gray-green and true silver, such interesting leaf shapes and forms of growth as the tiny white creeping antennarias, to tall sweeping branches of artemisias, and hoary, pointed junipers. The most critical eye must be charmed. Some of the leaves shine as though they were polished, others are wooly, or snowy; some are spidery in growth, others thick and heavy. One of our olives has silver-backed leaves that vary with the season from glistening white to mottled green. For color there are the shy blooms of lavenders, nepetas, sages, the brilliant cerise of the mullein pinks, the pure blue of the perovskia and the soft gold of yarrows. In late summer *Sedum seiboldi* turns pink-lined leaves to view in closely curled rosettes; later pink blossoms, like small brushes, remain until frost. For all the year, from earliest spring to the time when the snow covers the ground and decorates the junipers, the Silver Garden is richly rewarding, a gem setting of great beauty.

Leaves of lamb's-ear, here covered with dew, provide a soft silver accent wherever they grow.

Mrs. Simmons' Cabbage Patch

A very recent creation at Caprilands is a formal vegetable garden, known as Mrs. Simmons' Cabbage Patch. It is bordered with hundreds of parsleys and centered by a fig tree. The colors are an especially cooling treat in the summertime. Beds of cabbages are in shades of turquoise, purple and green. They are surrounded with purple and green basils. Flowering kales add additional color interest, as well as material for salads. The corner plantings are wormwood and the variety of texture is remarkable. The aroma of the basils in the hot summer sun is a treat in itself.

At right, *a fig tree is the central focus of Mrs. Simmons' Cabbage Patch.*

Cabbages grow in shades of turquoise, purple and green.

XIII

Capturing the World of Fragrance

Not all the ointments brought from Delos Ile,
Nor that of quinces, nor of marjoram,
That ever from the Ile of Coös came,
Nor these, nor any else, though ne'er so rare,
Could with this place for sweetest smells compare.
—*WILLIAM BROWNE*

The fragrant things of the world have romantic appeal—flowers, spices, aromatic gums, the resinous tree barks, even wet or burning leaves, the acrid odor of wood smoke, the earthy smell of new-turned soil—all touch the imagination. Spice may recall apple pie fresh from the oven or the different experience of incense in the gloom of a Gothic cathedral. The sweet breath of island paradises is caught in the scent of the fabulous clove. Fragrances have also proved to be the pot of gold at the foot of the rainbow. Continents have been discovered, islands colonized, industries developed, and fortunes made to insure the sources of such valued scent. The imagination of the churchman, of the lady of the manor, and the humble housewife have been stirred by the smell of incense, of strewing herbs, of medicinal plants. The merchant has found these a rich source of income, the apothecary has won fame by compounding them into love filters and charms for eternal youth; the priest has used them reverently in the rituals of worship.

Garden herbs have inspired churchmen, housewives, and merchants among others for hundreds of years.

A bridal bouquet created from the herb garden has special meaning and will be a lasting memento.

In stillrooms and apothecary shops, it was discovered that certain garden plants had odors similar to those of valuable spices. There were roses that smelled like cinnamon; and carnations with a scent like cloves. Since spices were clostly, it was desirable to extend them with herbal elements.

Ships brought strange gums, barks, beans, seed pods, even animal products to the apothecary. These provided fixatives for plant materials. The spice ball, the pomander, potpourris, and sweet bags with their combinations of spice and fruit scents were developed and preserved by the fixatives.

Ambergris, civet, and musk are three evil-smelling animal secretions that, with age, proper application, and blending give to perfumes a quality both rich and haunting. These were difficult ingredients to procure, so floral fixatives were sought and found in the root of the Florentine iris, patchouli leaves from Malay, tonka beans from South America and Africa, and vetiver roots from many places. These added a musky quality to mixtures. The lemon verbena plant from the Southwest, the new world of Spanish conquest, was brought to England in 1784 and added its fresh, cool lemon odor to many fragrant preparations.

Potpourri was originally not a luxury but a necessary nicety. In the days before good sanitation when fresh air was considered dangerous, castles and cottages alike needed the clean smell of flowers and the masking odor of spices. It was the duty of a proper housewife to make potpourris, sweet bags, and pomanders.

The rose jar was kept on the table in the best room, and, after the cleaning was done, it was opened and stirred to scent the room and freshen the air. Sweet bags, filled with lavender, lemon verbena, with herbs and spice mixtures, were fitted to the backs of chairs and placed in closets and linen presses. Sweet herbs were strewn on the floors of church and home to modify the accumulated odors of the rushes that covered the stone or earthen floors.

Many recipes for fragrances have been concocted. The lady of the manor, proud of her stillroom skill, spent hours compounding mixtures. Some of these recipes found their way into stillroom books and were treasured as family heirlooms. Others were included in popular herbals and are our common inheritance.

To walk in a garden of fragrant herbs is rewarding at any time of day, but to plant and tend such a garden is a rare pleasure indeed. Choosing plants that have sweet-smelling leaves and flowers that retain their odors is an interesting avocation, placing them in proper patterns, a fascinating occupation. To the herb gardener, there is also the reward of drying fragrant materials that will bring the garden inside for winter enjoyment.

The fragrant plants listed here can be grown in any garden that has some sun and a well-drained soil.

FRAGRANT LEAVES

Bay
Lavender
Lemon balm
Lemon geraniums
Lemon thyme
Lemon verbena
Narrowleaf French thyme
Orange mint
Oregano
Peppermint
Peppermint geraniums
Rose geraniums
Rosemary
Strawberry
Sweet basil
Sweet marjoram
Sweet woodruff
Tarragon

FRAGRANT SEEDS

Anise
Coriander
Fennel
Angelica

FRAGRANT PETALS

Lavender
Pinks
Roses

COLORFUL PETALS

Bachelor's-buttons
Blue salvia
Calendula
Daffodil
Delphinium
Forsythia
Lavender
Pansy
Pinks
Viola
Violet
Zonal geraniums

The seeds, leaves, bark, oil, roots and flowers of plants can all be sources of pleasing aromas.

Opposite, top, *fragrant plants will grow in any garden that has some sun and a well-drained soil.*

Spices for Potpourri

Allspice *(Pimenta dioica)* of the myrtle family grows naturally in the West Indies, especially Jamaica, and some trees are found in Mexico. The spice docks of Kingston are fragrant with this highly scented berry. Great casks of them fill the air with a wonderful odor not unlike bayrum.

Calamus root, and the oil derived from it, adds a mellow and somewhat spicy odor to potpourri. This product of *Acorus calamus* comes from France and Belgium.

Cinnamon barks or sticks (from *Cinnamomum zeylanicum*) of the laurel family yield a spicy element which was once the chief ingredient in the manufacture of the holy oils of the Bible. These were used for anointing priests and favored persons and the cleansing of the holy vessels. The cinnamon tree grows to 30 feet in nature; in cultivation it is a bush to be propagated from seeds. The young shoots are brilliant red, the bark speckled green and orange. Cinnamon is made from the inner bark which is cut in cylinders or quills from the time the trees are three or four years old; the best grade comes from young branches. India, Ceylon, Malaya, China, and the East Indies have groves of this beautiful tree.

I grind the stick cinnamon with whole cloves and add this coarse mixture to powdered orris root. Sometimes I grind a handful of tonka beans and mix this with the powdered frankincense and myrrh to make an excellent fixative. The mixture is stored in jars and sprinkled through the potpourri.

My recipe calls for ½ pound of stick cinnamon, 1 ounce tonka beans, 1 cup of powdered orris root with 10 drops rose oil, ½ cup of frankincense, and 1 tablespoon of myrrh.

Cloves (*Syzygium aromaticum,* of the myrtle family) come from trees 25 to 30 feet high that grow in Zanzibar, British Malaya, Ceylon, India, Madagascar, and Penang. Two annual harvests are made by the native villagers who pick the unexpanded flower buds by hand. The bunches are dried on mats, and the green buds removed from the stems. In about a week they are brown, ready to be sorted and graded for the market.

Frankincense *(Boswellia carteri)* gives us the most used and treasured of all the sweet odors from the East. Incense was a vital part of Hebrew worship, and several written versions of the temple mixtures are extant. The compounding of these was something of a secret and proportions were carefully weighed. One used four ingredients: stacte, onycha, galbanum, and frankincense. Another was comprised of thirteen elements, including myrrh, cassia, spikenard, saffron, costus, cinnamon, sweet bark, and an herb known as a "smoke raiser." The compounding was also a secret handed down through generations of incense makers. It is recorded that two pounds of incense were used every day in the temple in Jerusalem.

Frankincense in our time comes not only from Arabia, but from India, Ethiopia, and Somaliland. To procure the gum from which the essence of frankincense is obtained, incisions are made in the bark of the tree and the gum oozes out in large drops.

The odor of frankincense is not discernible in potpourri unless the mixture is warm or moist. However, it is a fixative and adds stability to a mixture. If you wish to enjoy something very fragrant, spinkle a little rose and spice potpourri with frankincense near hot coals in the fireplace. If you wish to burn frankincense and myrrh together, follow the old Hebrew rule of six parts of frankincense to one of myrrh.

Myrrh comes from a tree, *Commiphora myrrha,* that grows in Arabia, Ethiopia, and along the Somaliland Coast. Wood and bark are fragrant, and the gum flows slightly without cutting; it is dark brown and bitter tasting. In the past it was used to soothe a sore throat, for dentifrices, and as a purifying agent. The dead were embalmed with myrrh in Egypt and Palestine, and it was valued by Hebrews as a perfume. Kings, gods, and temples were censed with this distinctive gum from the time of the sun worshipers at Heliopolis, where it was burned daily at noon, until the reign of George III in England.

Patchouli *(Pogostemon cablin)* from Singapore, Sumatra, and British Malaya cannot be classified as a "spice," yet it is a fragrance that we import for potpourri. This is a tropical shrublike plant of the mint family with large musk-smelling dark leaves from which an essential oil was distilled in the 1850s, when it was a popular scent in Paris. The odor has been described as fruity, earthy, and of very warm character. I find that patchouli gives depth to potpourri, and has certain fixative powers as well.

When the bales of big patchouli leaves are first opened at Caprilands the odor is overpowering. A few leaves will scent a room and in my experience they never lose their odor. Patchouli and rose buds with orris root and a few drops of rose oil make a good mixture for a rose bowl to be left open. I add a large crushed leaf of patchouli to every rose jar as well as to each bag of potpourri.

At right, ***barn window shows off some items for sale in gift shop.*** Below, ***herb products provide enticing scents in the rooms of Caprilands.***

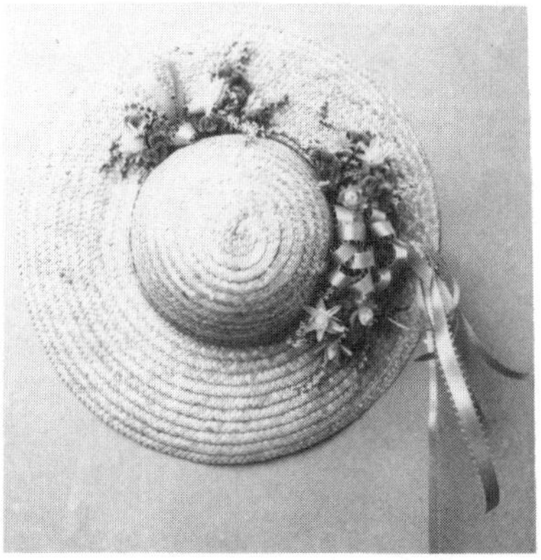

A decorated hat may be worn or displayed.

Sandalwood *(Santalum album)* grows 30 to 40 feet high, a native to the Malabar Coast, and found also in New Caledonia. From early time the wood was valued for its sweet odor and employed in the making of musical instruments, particularly those used in sacred ceremonies. It was also burned at sacrifices to idols and was later incorporated in incense for synagogues. There were domestic uses, too; fans were made of it and boxes lined as protection against moths.

Sandalwood chips are best for potpourri; they add that indefinable something that those who remember the old rose jars search for—sometimes in vain. For burning, both chips and larger pieces are effective. The chips mix well with other ingredients, such as frankincense, myrrh, vetiver, spices, and lavender flowers.

The tonka bean *(Dipteryx odorata),* sometimes called tonquin bean, provides one of the most concentrated of floral odors. It is overpowering in its sweetness, heavy with the smell of coumarin. The ground beans are important for good potpourri, since they act as fixative and an intensifier, sharpening other odors while losing their own identity. Beans are imported from Brazil, Ceylon, Venezuela, British Guiana, and Africa.

Vetiver root *(Vetiveria zizanioides)* comes mainly from Java and the Reunion Islands, small amounts from Louisiana and the West Indies. Vetiver is an 8-foot grass in its native climate. It has a fragrant root with the odor of violets or sandalwood. As a fixative in potpourri, it never seems to lose its fragrance, although this is more noticeable in a warm, moist atmosphere. In the South, vetiver root is put in bureau drawers and closets to keep away moths and ants and to scent clothing. It is effective as incense and at its best in oriental mixtures.

Fixatives to Hold Flower Fragrances

Fixatives from the animal or plant world are used to hold the fragrance of potpourri ingredients. Animal fixatives include ambergris, civet, and musk. Ambergris is a substance from the intestines of the sperm whale, and it is found on beaches or floating on waters of the South Seas. The odor is disagreeable, but like many fixatives, when combined with fragrant things, it absorbs and enhances the essences.

The plant fixatives I use most are orris root, and tonka bean. Orris root comes from *Iris florentina,* a variety of *I. germanica.* The fresh root is dug, peeled and sun-dired, then stored for two years to develop the scent. It is then ground and emits the violet odor for which it is known. Orris root is the most common fixative for potpourri as it is easily obtainable. I use it generously, at least 1 cup to 1 pound of rose petals, along with spices and other essences.

Oils Essential for Potpourri

When essences or essential oils are included in recipes, the distilled plant oil is indicated. These are generally volatile oils that evaporate at room temperatures. They occur in secretory cells, reservoirs, glands of flowers, barks, fruits, and leaves. Most oils are obtained by steam distillation.

Attar of roses is the most fabulous and desirable of all oils. There is a charming story of the origin of attar of roses in the year 1562, the time of the Grand Moguls. For the wedding of Princess Nour-Djihan to the Emperor Djihangugr all pathways the royal pair would use were strewn with the sweet roses of the East. The canals surrounding the palaces were so filled with roses that the royal barges could scarcely be propelled through the floating petals.

Spice packets contain potpourri and make welcome small gifts.

In the heat of the day, bride and groom sought refuge in the royal barge. As they drifted along, the princess noticed a thin film upon the water. She trailed her hand in it and found it slick with an oil sweet beyond belief. This was indeed the very essence of the rose. Her discovery, carried to the royal apothecary, resulted in the valuable oil of roses.

The first rose oils came from the East. At one time rose perfume was the only one known. Rose water was first made and recorded in the eleventh century by Avicenna, a Persian Moslem of unusual intellect and learning. Rose oil was first made by steeping roses in oil, not by distillation. Much of the attar of roses produced later came from Bulgaria, out of the famous Valley of the Roses where the *Rosa damascena,* a native of the Orient introduced into Europe during the Crusades, was cultivated by hundreds of rose farmers. Many of them distilled their own essences in old-fashioned stills. It is said that it takes ten thousand pounds of rose petals to make one pound of oil. Hence the high cost of attar of roses, or "rose otto" as it is sometimes called.

Other oils used in the making of potpourri include oil of violet, carnation, jasmine, lemon verbena, and orange blossom.

When to Make Potpourri

Through the summer and far into autumn, the good herb gardener is busy harvesting. Airtight tin containers hold chip-dry rose petals, aromatic lavender, lemon verbena, orange mint, and others of the mint family. Large boxes or drawers in an old dresser hold a colorful selection of dried flowers, not necessarily fragrant, for decoration within the glass jars of potpourri. When gardening demands are less strenuous, there is no task quite so pleasant as the making of potpourri.

Recipes for Potpourri

Lemon Verbena Jar

- 1 cup dried lemon verbena leaves
- 1 cup dried lemon balm leaves
- rind of 1 lemon, dried and grated
- ½ cup each dried petals from forsythia, calendula, lemon-scented dwarf marigold
- 1 ounce orris root with 6 drops of lemon verbena oil
- leaves of lemon-scented thyme, optional

Combine all ingredients, then turn into small apothecary jars. Press some of the yellow flowers against the sides of the jar for color. Tie the top with yellow and green velvet ribbon.

Potpourri of Herbs and Flowers

- 1 cup each of dried thyme, orange mint, and bergamot leaves
- 1 cup of mixed dried blossoms
- ¼ cup each of dried tarragon and rosemary
- 1 ounce orris root with 6 drops of oil of bergamot

Prepare as for lemon verbena jar; tie with a ribbon of appropriate color.

Moist Potpourri

- 3 cups dried rose petals
- 1 cup bay salt
- 1 teaspoon each of allspice, cinnamon, and coriander
- 1 tablespoon each of cloves, grated nutmeg, and anise
- 1 cup dried lavender
- ¼ cup each of patchouli leaves and powdered orris root
- ¼ ounce each of oil of rose and oil of rose geranium
- 3 cups of a mixture made of dried rosemary, lemon balm, and lemon verbena leaves

In a covered crock, mix rose petals with the bay salt and leave for one week, turning daily. Add spices and let stand for another week, turning daily. At the end of the two weeks add the lavender, patchouli, orris root, and oils. Let stand for a few weeks, then mix in leaves of dried rosemary, lemon balm, and lemon verbena. Stir frequently with a wooden spoon or cinnamon stick.

Rose Jar

Mix first eight ingredients thoroughly; then add the rose oil and orris root. Mix again and stir well. If this amount of orris seems excessive, remember that this is a basic mixture to which you can add flowers of the season right up to fall. After it is finished, close the jar for at least two weeks (a month is better), then it will be ready to enjoy.

- 1 quart dried rose petals
- 1 cup each of dried lavender flowers and rose geranium leaves
- ½ cup patchouli
- ¼ cup of sandalwood chips and vetiver, mixed
- 2 teaspoons of frankincense and myrrh, mixed
- 1 teaspoon each of powdered benzoin, cinnamon, and cloves
- 2 tonka beans, ground
- ¼ cup allspice
- 10 drops rose oil
- 1 cup orris root

Mint Potpourri

Combine ingredients and store in apothecary jars. When you are entertaining, turn some of this mixture out into a pewter or silver bowl. Stir it slightly and the smell of a fresh clean breeze will permeate the room. An excellent potpourri for a desk or worktable, perhaps in a widemouth, antique sugarbowl of stoneware or old blue Staffordshire.

- 2 cups dried lavender
- 1 cup dried mint leaves (peppermint, spearmint, or orange mint)
- ½ cup dried culinary thyme
- ¼ cup rosemary
- few drops of essential oils of lavender, thyme, and bergamot
- dried red geranium petals, blue bachelor's-button, and delphinium

Potpourri of Herbs, Flowers, and Citrus

Prepare as for lemon verbena jar.

- 6 cups dried rose petals
- 1 cup each of dried culinary thyme (preferably narrowleaf French), rosemary, sweet marjoram, lavender, and sweet basil (narrowleaf bush)
- 6 crushed bay leaves
- 1 tablespoon allspice, crushed
- rind of 1 orange and 1 lemon, dried and crushed
- 1 teaspoon anise seed

It is always a matter of surprise and perhaps disappointment to the novice to discover that while the chief ingredient of potpourri is the rose, much of its lasting fragrance comes from exotic materials that bring out, preserve, and add to the basic scent. A bushel of carefully dried petals, tinned and stored in a dry, cool place, will emit an odor like tea with very little sweetness. This is partly due to the difficulty of getting the old fragrant damask roses, partly because few remember what went into Grandmother's rose jar.

Plan to add many ingredients to your potpourri. Get them well in advance and make your mixture by late November so that it can ripen for one month before being transferred to jars or bags for gifts.

How to Make Sachets and Scented Pillows

Sachets are made simply by tying up a fragrant dried mixture of potpourri in a square of organdy or fine net. Decorate with little dried roses or everlastings and a bow. Antique glass containers with a sachet in them make delightful gifts.

Covers for scented pillows are made of organdy, fine net, or silk; but put the more sturdy fragrances of pine and patchouli into soft felt or homespun. Pieces of brocade, velvet, and chintz also make useful covers. For these small pillows, make an attractive case of one of these materials and a slightly smaller lining of muslin to hold the fragrant mixture.

Use prolific plants from the herb garden for the bulk of fragrant material for pillows. Lemon balm is one of the most leafy herbs; lemon and camphor southernwoods also produce an abundance of foliage with a clean, penetrating and lasting scent. Combine any of these with cuttings of rosemary, bergamot, thyme, and bay leaves, and a generous amount of dried orange and lemon peel.

Below, ***statice, or other everlastings, when dried can be used to decorate sachets.*** Below right, ***southernwood is used for bulk in potpourri mixtures.***

Autumn

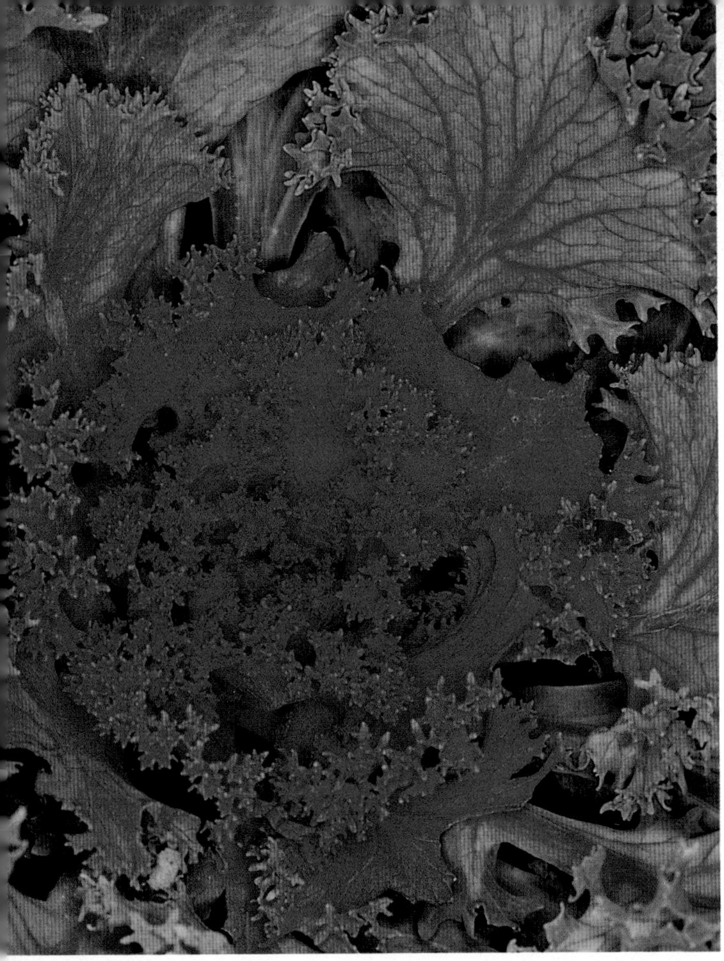

Flowering kale can be counted on as a source of fall color.

Salad burnet grows profusely in late summer and fall.

Preserved herbs come in many colors and textures.

Fall visitors stroll the stone walkways in the gardens.

A swag in fall colors is a lovely accent over a doorway or mantel.

Flowers common along the roadside make attractive bouquets.

XIV

Autumn Diary

For there is hope of a tree, if it be cut down, that it will sprout again, and that the tender branch thereof will not cease.

—JOB 14:7

The herb garden in autumn has a special charm. Now that the competition of surrounding flower gardens is banished by frost, the calm beauty of massed plantings of greens and grays is seen at its best. Now is the time to appreciate leaf formation, texture, and the distinctive growth that marks a green garden for contemplation, a place where delightful odors, pungent, sweet, and heady, carry us back the remarkable way that only odors can do.

The gray border garden at Caprilands is planted in a semicircle around a weathered shrine. Here a medieval figure of Virgin and Child smile on herbs arranged in formal half-moon beds. These look fresh until late December. The back border of *Artemisia albula* is stark white against the blue fall sky, or a ghostly shadow in the light of the hunters' moon.

Close to the shrine a variety of santolina makes miniature round trees with leaves like silver filigree. Tall, tangerine-scented branches of southernwood wave gracefully about the shrine. Mats of gray thyme interspersed with golden thyme emphasize the year-round color of this garden: gray, green, gold, and white. Two semicircular beds in the center are separated by walks of old brick bounded with soft masses of easy-growing lamb's-ears *(Stachys olympica)*. The whole border is edged with lacy Roman wormwood *(Artemisia pontica),* kept reasonably trim by cutting back twice a year, and by pulling roots to keep lines even. Santolina, also called lavender-cotton, forms a chain of white coral-like growth the whole length of the garden.

Some beds are bordered with sage, two with camphor-scented southernwood, others with hyssop and rue. Snow-on-the-mountain *(Euphorbia marginata)* falls in gray cascades over the walls and draws attention to a small rock garden below, where rows of *Artemisia* Silver Mound make silk cushions. Bushes of hyssop are still in bloom, and pot-marigolds *(Calendula officinalis)* are tossing heads of yellow and deep orange, untouched by frost, against the cloud of *Artemisia* Silver King.

In the thyme terrace below the border garden, armies of Johnny-jump-ups are awake after a summer sleep, ready for winter blooming. Sweet alyssum is foaming in fragrant waves all through the garden. Costmary or Bible leaf *(Chrysanthemum balsamita)* has a fine second blooming and looks up over the bank toward the tawny plumes of its more glamorous relatives, the chrysanthemums. Thymes are at their greenest and grayest now, reaching out exploring arms to anchor safely under protecting rocks for the winter. Many have late blooms. Mother-of-thyme often blooms for Thanksgiving.

Another name for the calendula is pot-marigold.

An espaliered apple tree shows careful pruning.

To walk among these herbs on a late November day is an adventure. The day should be sunny with the frosty mist of autumn hanging over the hills, shutting you and the garden into gratifying solitude. The smell of the damp earth, the mingled fragrance of thymes, mints, and lavenders rises with every step, and your eye is held by garden beauty in somber key.

Autumnal Caprilands is a season with many facets of interest and meaning. The shorter, darker days are interspersed with hours of brilliant sun that end with white cold moonlit nights, when one suspects ghosts will be stealing through the ravaged garden and the wail of lost spirits will ride the wind. Modern lighting does not even completely break the spell, for the scent of autumn and the dying year is in the air and it casts a curtain of magic over the most mundane tasks and pleasures. Cutting a long row of sage, picking pungent pennyroyal, gathering marigolds for table bouquets, their odor ever reminiscent of fall, bunching thyme for hanging, and stripping the fernlike tansy leaves and the bitter wormwood, all these tasks, our regular autumn work, become touched with a ritual feeling, for old magic is in the air, and marks this season from all others. It is at this time that

Autumn harvest is a time of long days of gathering mature herbs.

the first spell of woodsmoke from the great old fireplace scents the air like rising incense and burns as a tribute to the gods of autumn and the harvest—a special libation to the house gods who keep us warm in winter. After the hard labor of the day there's a little time to sit and remember, savoring the eerie delights of late fall afternoons. It's a time to tell tales, to work charms, to listen to voices from the past. Fortunate we are, that we live so close to nature; all our working days are spent in growing, cultivating, harvesting and using the herbs of the garden and the field. Evenings are spent in discovery of plant histories that add to the fascination of our gardening life.

As we bring in the sheaves of new blossoming calendulas with their gold and orange disks like lighted suns, and as we hang the long strands of orange bittersweet from the worn beams in our living room ceiling, as we pick the wonderful smelly marigolds, and the bronze chrysanthemums with their daisy-like odor to combine with the moonstruck artemisia, we are reminded that all the flowers with orange and yellow tones of the season were protective plants against the evil charms of witchcraft, for their hot colors represent the fires which any careful witch would avoid.

XV

The Artemisias, the Glory of Autumn

What savour is best, if physic be true,
for places infacted than wormwood and rue?
It is as a comfort, for heart and the brain,
and therefore to have it, it is not in vain.
—THOMAS TUSSER

To the herb gardener, the words artemisia and autumn are synonymous. I could add another alliterative *A*, for art goes along with them, too, because of their many uses in landscapes and arrangements. Properly managed, artemisias can be the backbone of a well-planned herb garden; however, they cannot be counted on for early spring, as many do not develop fully until August. Then they become the glory of autumn, providing accents and graceful patterns both day and night.

Belonging to the composite family, artemisias are generally divided into four groups: mugworts, wormwoods, southernwoods, and decorative types. Tarragon *(Artemisia dracunculus sativus)* stands alone as it is primarily a seasoning herb. The confusing nomenclature of artemisias is sufficient to drive one to madness, but the poet Andrew Fletcher wrote,

These for frenzy be
A speedy and a sovereign remedy,
The bitter wormwood, sage and marigold.

In the fall the artemesias are at their fullest.

Authorities differ on the origin of the name "artemisia." I have always accepted the explanation that, since the artemisias, particularly the mugwort or *A. vulgaris* type, and the wormwoods were used for women and their many ailments, these plants took the name from Artemis or Diana, goddess of the hunt, of the moon, and of virginity. The moon is a fitting patroness for artemisias as they are at their best in the light of a harvest moon, or in the cold white nights of November when the last wispy stalks wave their goodby to the old year.

Decorating with Artemisias

To make an artemisia tree, cut Silver King when it is completely headed, probably in the middle of September. Try to cut just before the brownish seed heads have formed so that the plants will dry white and not be woolly. Dry only overnight or not at all, as the plant is stiff and will be more workable if not dried. Make a half or full circle of chicken wire 6 inches across. Half trees made on a semicircular, cone-shaped frame are more practical than full-circle ones, as they do not require as much material or space.

Start the tree with the best, most perfectly formed and upright bush of artemisia. Fix this in the wire for the main trunk. Place two lesser stalks in opposite directions and at right angles to the trunk. Let these rest on the table to give stability, and place so that the ends curl. Then proceed up the sides of the tree. Put the branches into the wire or into other interlaced branches, as they will soon hold each other. Always turn the curls up and break off any branches that you will not be using so that a thick, unmanageable mass does not build up.

The finished tree can be 18 to 36 inches high, made on the same frame. Larger artemisia trees take an enormous amount of material—cuttings from about six large plants—while small trees can be made from one well-grown plant.

Each year I add to my stored trees, keeping the basic materials, which I wash under the kitchen faucet to remove dust, dry slightly, and to which I add fresh artemisia. This saves the long first process. Some mantel trees are made with scraps or the lovely tops of silver that are already miniature trees without effort on my part.

To decorate an artemisia tree for autumn, I use the full-blown chartreuse ambrosia. If the tree is made in early fall, the ambrosia will be easy to work with, somewhat sticky, pliable and very fragrant. Fresh tansy heads picked when they are bright yellow and fully formed add more color to the trim. Oregano blossoms yield a rich brown, green, or purple, depending on when they are picked and how they are dried. Roadside everlastings *(Gnaphalium obtusifolium)* impart a soft flowery texture to the decoration, and tiny spruce cones may be wired into the branches. Bright yellow blossoms of yarrow lift up the deeper tones of the tansy. White yarrow and bits of baby's-breath may also be added. The trees are best if kept to autumn tones—greens, browns, and yellows—or made white and gold with the addition of gilded leaves and cones for Christmas. I sometimes gild the small rose hips from *Rosa chinensis* (hedge rose) as they are in proportion to the rest of the decoration. The trees look best if left quite natural; artificial decorations are to be avoided. This should be an herbal tree, made from the harvest of your garden.

The Caprilands artemesia harvest must be profuse because great amounts are required for holiday decorations.

Teasel burrs, picked already dry along roadsides, have many decorative uses.

Swags of artemisia are fixed to our worn red doors on the first of October. They include harvest corn, a sign of hospitality, and branches of rue to "ward off evil and the attacks of witches." Fresh-cut branches of rue dry to brilliant green. A branch of elder and large umbels of dill also "hinder witches of their will," and rosettes of pine cones tightly wired make a firm center motif.

To make a swag, place large well-headed sprays of Silver King, with tops going in opposite directions, and bend the tops to a semicircle. Bind stems together in the center. Then wire in other sprays of artemisia down the sides. Long sprays of mugwort and wormwood blossoms are decorative when placed to follow the lines of the basic Silver King and contribute their own symbolic protection and good fortune. A large rosette of cones wired firmly together can be used with the Indian corn hanging as a pendant below, or teasels may be inserted at the top and bottom of the design with rose hips in the center. Christmas swags are made for inside decoration much the same way as the autumn ones, but then they are often background for a string of bells. I add dull green, brown, or gold velvet ribbon. These swags stand like gray lace against the deep reds of the walls or the black panels of the old doors. They are truly elegant and can be used to good effect in most settings.

Statice, yarrow and celosia decorate this wreath.

XVI

Harvest Party

"The spirits of the air live on the smells
of fruit; and Joy, with pinions light, roves round
The gardens, or sits singing in the trees,"
Thus sang the jolly Autumn as he sat;
Then rose, girded himself, and o'er the bleak
Hills fled from our sight; but left his golden load.
—*WILLIAM BLAKE*

St. Michael's Day, September 29, is a delightful time for a party. There is a hint of autumn in the air though days are still warm and sunny. Basil rows are full and fragrant in the sun, green and purple against the long background of gray artemisias. Unharvested savory is in blossom, reddish now in leaves and stems, and covered with minute white blooms. Mints sprawl along the paths, and thymes have burst all bounds, spilling onto driveways and over the lawn where the mower cuts a fragrant path.

Everywhere the harvest is ready. The kitchen rafters are hung with drying mint for winter tea, with bunches of sage for holiday seasonings, and flowers to add color to winter arrangements. The air is filled with good harvest smells and with the opening of the ktichen door the heady incense of heated spice and baking bread is wafted through the house.

This is the incense burned for St. Michael, patron of soldiers, coopers, hatmakers, haberdashers, and grocers, the saint of the great soldier-lords of the manors, of the middle-class merchants and purveyors of food. St. Michael is one of the three archangels mentioned in the Scriptures who appears with a flaming sword to protect Christians from the snares of the devil and to lead them to light eternal. The pagan gods Mercury and Wotan were ousted from their high places by the Christian Michael. His most famous deed was the raising of his flaming sword against the plague in Rome. One of the most beautiful of all churches, Mont St. Michel in Normandy, was built in his honor and has survived countless wars and changes, remaining a shrine for Christians everywhere.

St. Michael's Day was celebrated throughout Europe. This was the end of the harvest time in medieval Europe, when herds were driven home from mountain pastures, when laborers hired on St. George's Day (April 23) were given wages and discharged after much feasting and gaiety. Many left with a gift of a live squealing pig under their arms or a roast of pork, a fresh ham, or a goose. Pork and goose were the foods used for the feasting and the outdoor spits turned all day in their preparation.

In French cities the pancake-maker was busy on St. Michael's Day at his place in the shadow of the great cathedrals, for it was his business to make a sweet, crisp cake, much like a waffle, called *gaufre.* The long-handled iron pan in which he baked the cake over a charcoal fire had beautiful religious designs embossed in it and these left their imprint on the waffle. The iron pans are collectors' items today.

The varied herb harvest can fill a window.

In Scotland St. Michael's Day was remembered with a rich fruit cake called St. Michael's Bannock. This was made with wild and cultivated fruits and a mixture of all the harvest grains, oats, rye, and barley, a multitude of eggs and much butter and cream, with honey for sweetening. All represented the bounty of nature and the richness of the harvest.

Even brooms can be festive.

Recipes for Autumn

Thus our theme is set by the harvest festivals of the past for a Michaelmas Festival. The recipes for his harvest party are my adaptation of the traditional meats and sweets served as the bounty of St. Michael.

The punch bowl stands in the center of an old barrel head in which ivies grow happily through the year in sphagnum moss; for special days we insert other plants in this green circle. Woodruff grows around the May bowl, thymes and mints decorate midsummer parties, and in the fall mints are supplemented with Michaelmas daisies, cut and inserted in the moist moss. The punch bowl rises like a white flower out of this mass of fragrant green.

Traditionally this harvest festival was celebrated with libations of foaming ale and various types of home-brew, but our guests prefer a more delicate refreshment.

Traditional fall decorations are part of the scene.

Recipes for a Harvest Party

Caprilands Chile Bean Pot

- 2 28-ounce cans red kidney beans
- ¼ cup basil or garlic vinegar
- ½ cup chutney or tomato preserve
- 1 large clove garlic, crushed
- 3 green rosemary tips, or ¼ teaspoon dried rosemary
- 2 teaspoons chili powder
- 6 whole cloves
- 1 teaspoon dry mustard, or 2 tablespoons herb mustard
- 2 bay leaves
- ½ teaspoon dried thyme
- ½ teaspoon basil
- 2 large onions, sliced
- ½ cup strong black decaffeinated coffee

Combine all ingredients except onions in a 3-quart beanpot and on top arrange onions. Cook at 350° until liquid is thickened, 3 or 4 hours. Half an hour before serving, remove beanpot from oven and pour in ½ cup of strong black decaffeinated coffee.
Serves 8 to 10.

Fruit Gingerbread with Coriander

- 1¼ cups unbleached white flour
- 1¼ cups whole wheat flour
- 2 teaspoons baking soda
- ¼ pound (1 stick) butter
- ¼ cup honey
- 1 cup molasses
- 2 eggs, lightly beaten
- 1 cup boiling water
- 2 teaspoons ground ginger
- 1 teaspoon cinnamon
- 1 teaspoon ground cloves
- ½ teaspoon ground coriander
- ½ cup raisins
- ½ cup walnuts, chopped
- ¼ cup dried peaches (optional), chopped

Preheat oven to 350°. Sift together flours and baking soda. Set aside. Cream butter with honey and molasses. Add eggs and beat until fluffy. Mix in boiling water. Add flour mixture and spices and beat until well blended. Stir in raisins, walnuts and peaches. Pour batter into a greased 9×9-inch pan and baked at 350° for 45 minutes.
Serves 12.

Caprilands Cheese Rolls

Preheat oven to 350°. Place cheese in a medium bowl. Crumble the herbs between your palms and add them to the cheese. Add the garlic and mix well. Sift together flours and baking powder. Cut in the butter, then add the milk and stir until well mixed. Roll the dough on a well-floured surface into a 6 × 24-inch rectangle. Sprinkle the cheese mixture evenly over the dough, leaving a ½ inch border on each long side. Brush one exposed border with cold water. Starting at the opposite side, roll the dough up jelly roll style. (The water will seal the outside edge.) Cut the roll into 1-inch-thick slices, and arrange the slices about 1 inch apart on greased cookie sheets. Bake at 350° for about 25 minutes or until done.
Yields 2 dozen rolls.

- ½ pound sharp cheddar cheese, grated
- 1 teaspoon dried oregano
- ½ teaspoon dried rosemary
- 1 teaspoon dried sage
- 1 clove garlic, minced
- 1½ cups unbleached white flour
- 1½ cups whole wheat flour
- 4 teaspoons baking powder
- ¼ pound (1 stick) butter
- ¾ cup milk

Autumn Red Punch

Marinate the burnet, which has a cucumber flavor, and the thyme in the grape and orange juice for about 4 hours, allowing the mixture to stand at room temperature. Toss peaches with honey. Arrange the peaches and the grapes over a flat cake of ice. Pour the juice mixture over the fruit. Have extra quartered peaches and grapes ready for second servings.
Makes 20 punch-cup servings.

- 24 sprigs burnet, bruised
- 1 sprig thyme, to cut sweetness
- 2 quarts grape juice
- 2 cups orange juice
- ½ cups honey
- 6 ripe peaches, peeled and quartered
- 2 bunches green grapes, separated
- 1 bunch purple grapes, separated
- flat cake of ice

Brown Autumn Cookies

Preheat oven to 350°. First combine the flours, butter, and 2 tablespoons brown sugar. Pat into a well-greased 9 × 13-inch pan. Bake in a 350° oven for 10 minutes. Next beat eggs to a froth and mix with the 1 cup honey, coconut, raisins, walnuts, and herb seeds. Stir in lemon juice and rind. Spread this egg mixture over the slightly cooled baked mixture in the pan. Bake 25 minutes. When cool, cut into squares.
Makes 2 dozen cookies.

- 1 cup whole wheat flour
- 1 cup unbleached white flour
- ½ cup butter
- 2 tablespoons brown sugar
- 3 eggs
- 1 cup honey
- 1 cup shredded unsweetened coconut
- 1 cup raisins
- ½ cup chopped walnuts
- 2 tablespoons sesame seeds
- 1 tablespoon caraway seeds
- 2 caradamom seeds, shelled and crushed
- 2 tablespoons lemon juice
- 1 teaspoon grated lemon rind

XVII

Harvesting and Preserving Herbs

And on his left he held a basketfull
Of all sweet herbs that searching eye could cull:
Wild Thyme, and valley-lilies whiter still
Than Leda's love, and cresses from the rill.
—*JOHN KEATS*

Drying home-grown herbs is one of the great pleasures of herb gardening. It is rewarding to use your own fresh seasonings, and if you dry them, you will doubly appreciate each savory leaf. Drying processes are simple, and the work need not be done all at once for plants mature at different times. Almost all herbs produce two, sometimes three, crops beginning in midsummer if they are harvested frequently.

The best time to cut plants for seasoning is before noon after the dew has dried but before the sun has leached the essential oils that keep herbs fresh and flavorsome. Of course, herbs should be dried out of direct sun.

Cut the leafy herbs, such as basil, savory, chervil, and marjoram, just before blossoms form. After blooming, leaves change color in some varieties; savory becomes very dark and the already-small leaves look black and shriveled when dried. This doesn't mean that leaves cannot be cut from these plants *after* blooming. If you do forget them, don't despair. They will still be full of flavor, though their color and texture will not be perfect.

Leafy herbs should be harvested before blossoms form.

Where to Dry the Herb Harvest

Dry herbs in the shade, but not in a damp place. Sometimes in very dry weather an outdoor shed can be used, but moisture will seep in at night and drying will be slowed. For best color, quick drying is advisable, but heat should not exceed 150 degrees. One method is to spread leaves thinly on a tray of fine wire mesh. This tray is placed in a slow oven with the door left open. Watch carefully as drying should be completed within a matter of minutes, the time dependent on the thickness of the leaves.

Herbs are decorative hung in bunches from ceiling rafters to dry, or strung on a pole across the front of a fireplace, the original way of curing them. You can still dry herbs by these old-fashioned methods, as long as you do not leave them hanging so long that they pick up dust. Brown paper bags may be used for drying but many holes will have to be punched in them to let air in and moisture out. Brown wrapping paper spread on boards in an attic or an unused room works well as a base on which to dry herbs. Spread out the stems in a single layer on top of paper to allow for air circulation. Of course the attic, or what used to be known as the "woodshed chambers" in Vermont, where my grandmother's sage for sausage was always drying, is ideal. Few modern houses have attics or other space to be used for long-time drying, however, so the quick method is usually best.

A few herbs need no washing before drying, especially if the garden rows where they grow are mulched thickly with salt hay. However, I wash all leaves excepting those of herbs gathered for seeds, and an occasional tall mint. Small herbs that grow close to the ground, such as marjoram, parsley, and thyme and those with thick, wrinkled leaves, like horehound and sage, need special treatment and go through three waters before they are ready for drying. The warm water bath is first, then cool water rinses and draining on a screen in the sink before leaves are put into the drying rack. Washing needs to be done quickly, as warm water releases oils and flavor may be lost if the leaves stay wet for very long.

Herbs to dry in trays include chervil, lovage, myrrh, lemon verbena, parsley, thyme, and rosemary. Leaves of parsley and lovage are so thick that they can be spread only one layer deep. Thyme, on the other hand, holds so little moisture that a basket may be piled full and it will dry well in any place that is not damp. Lemon verbena leaves are

Chive blossoms may be cut and dried for winter bouquets.

usually removed separately when plants are brought in for the winter. It is wise to take leaves from plants at this time, as they will drop as soon as they are brought inside, and they may be lost or soiled if they fall of their own accord. Dried rosemary needles are sharp if left whole; I run these through a coffee grinder and they emerge at just about the right length for coating a chicken, seasoning a gravy, or spooning out for tea.

Cockscomb celosia grows in several colo

Herbs that dry well hanging in bunches include sage, savory, mint, oregano, marjoram, basil, lemon balm, and horehound. If the bunches of basil are too large, leaves blacken quickly; the flavor will be there if they do not mold, but the color will be unattractive. Dill may be dried in this fashion if the green leaves are desired. In a warm room all these plants dry in two days, sometimes overnight in my kitchen, but our stove burns constantly, and the kitchen is dry even in humid weather.

Chives needs to be cut or shredded for drying. If you have plenty, perhaps a border in your kitchen garden, you will cut it back as the season advances but be sure to let a border of it blossom. Cut and dry some for winter bouquets. When blooms left on plants begin to fade, pull out the flowering stalks and cut the whole plant back to the ground. Chives require much sorting as some leaves yellow quickly and only the tender green ones are of value. Cut these into pieces about half an inch long or finer. I put these into baskets hung over my stove and they are ready to package in about two days. I dry dill in much the same way, cutting it into bits while it is green. This is one of winter's most useful seasonings.

Herb seeds to dry include those of coriander, cumin, caraway, dill, and fennel. Watch these carefully or seeds will fall and be lost. Cut the whole plant, and place it, seed head down, in a paper bag so as to catch all the seeds. Hang up until dry and the seeds will drop out readily. As these seed herbs mature at different times, caraway not until the second year, you will have to be vigilant to save your harvest.

Some herb gardeners find pleasure in pressing leaves and flowers between folds of parchment or old Bibles just like the ancient specimens in herbariums. These old dried pieces often retain characteristic shapes and odors, reminding us as we open the books in winter of bright summer days in the garden. Some of my friends make their own designs for notepaper with pressed pieces of herbs, and it is pleasant to open a letter with leaves and flowers placed in interesting designs. There is something magical about a little grouping of herbs, no matter how humble or how dry they may be. Each year I press dozens of costmary leaves (known as Bible leaf) in our heaviest books, and use them in collections of Biblical herbs at Christmas. Pick costmary all summer in order to get leaves in good condition. They need no special drying; just choose perfect leaves and press them in a heavy book or between pieces of newspaper weighted down by a brick.

Plume celosia can be used for color in sizeable arrangements of dried material.

Sweet geranium leaves also make good bookmarks and retain fragrance better than other plants. For bookmarks, I like the cutleaf forms of Dr. Livingston, the fernleaf, old-fashioned rose, and many of the variations. The leaves of lamb's-ears are also easily pressed. Mullein leaves and rosettes cut through the summer and put under heavy pressure are useful in winter arrangements.

I also press thyme, bedstraw, rosemary, and pennyroyal, which with costmary leaves, are used in Christmas crêche decorations or sent in little cellophane packages to friends during the holidays. These are all picked in summer, pressed, and put away for future use. Cards with the story and symbols of each herb make distinctive Christmas remembrances.

Many herbs can be dried for winter arrangements. I try anything from my garden or the roadside that looks interesting. Plants I recommend highly include amaranth, ambrosia, artemisia, bachelor's-button, broom, delphinium, globe amaranth, helichrysum, lamb's-ears, lanceleaf goldenrod, lavender, mullein, oregano, peppermint, perilla, red orach, statice, St. John's-wort, sorrel seed heads, tansy, teasel, woad, and yarrow.

When I gather foliage and flowers for drying, I often find dried seed pods that are interesting for arrangements. Some of these I wait to gather after frost, others I pick at various times from midsummer on. Searching for interesting herb seed pods for arrangements is a fascinating business. I look for agrimony, baptisia, broom, flax, horehound, Japanese iris, lily, okra, peppergrass, rose hips, rue, shepherd's-purse, thermopsis, and veronica.

How to Store Dried Herbs

The faster herbs are processed, the better. If they hang too long they will lose flavor. Have clean glass screw-top jars all ready or, if you cannot process immediately, leave stems on and store in a large, airtight metal container. Herbs keep better on stems. If leaves are pulled off and shredded, they must be bottled at once to preserve the essential oil that determines flavor.

Herbs need to be "chip dry" when they are processed. Strip the leaves of thyme and savory, crumble those of basil. I do not powder herbs, as the oils in whole leaves or parts of large leaves keep better. I use an old-fashioned corn grinder, just right to break up a leaf without powdering it. Parsley may be prepared this way, or put through a coarse sieve, as for basils. Most leaves I leave whole, but I grind some for special uses. Handling tends to destroy flavor, so put the finished product in jars at once and screw on the tops. Work in a dry place and check jars for moisture. If any shows on the glass, remove the herbs at once and dry them again or all your efforts will be lost. Green herbs must be kept out of strong light or sun, for the color fades quickly. Store in a closed cupboard.

Leafy herbs, such as basil, are best if stored for no more than one year in dried form, and should be kept in a closed cupboard to prevent their color from fading.

Keep seed herbs in their original form until they are to be used. Ground coriander and cardamom deteriorate rapidly, but if the seeds are stored whole they keep indefinitely. If you wish, powder or crush these just before using with a rolling pin or use time-proven mortar and pestle. Almost all left-over herb seeds will germinate if planted out the next year. Excess seed also makes good winter bird food.

Leafy herbs need to be renewed after one year, but seed herbs are good for several years if containers are tightly closed.

Storing herbs for flower arrangements is less complicated than for kitchen herbs. It is important after they are dried to keep them in a dry, airy, dustfree place. As the branches cure, they get brittle, and require careful handling. They can be left in bunches hanging from a ceiling if covered with polyethylene plastic to protect them from dust. Or stand bunches in boxes and baskets, and cover with a large sheet of thin plastic.

Freezing Herbs

Freezing is a simple process and most effective for sorrel, basil, parsley, dill, chives and chervil. Wash these lightly, then place on paper towels to drain and dry thoroughly. Do not blanch these leafy herbs (This has a tendency to make them soft and it is not necessary). Freeze separate leaves or whole branches in plastic bags as you do with parsley. Do not overcrowd the herbs, and be sure you lay them flat. Keep them frozen until time to use them. It is best to determine how much is usually used at a time in order not to waste the precious leaves. Do not try to do too much at one time. Herbs that are commonly used together may be frozen in the same packages. Be sure that you label each kind and pack them together. Unless you are very accustomed to their appearances, they can be confusing.

One of our assistants, whose experience with herbs is of long standing, suggests freezing parsley in a ball and shaving off the desired amount as it is needed. Another, who cooks for her family and uses basil, finds freezing the leaves flat in small packages or in cakes and cutting off the amount to be used a workable method. Dried basil has a distinctly different flavor; frozen basil has a more natural fresh garden taste. Freezing herbs in cubes of ice is recommended if you will be using them in small quantities. The cube when removed from the

Parsley may be stored by freezing in cubes of ice.

freezer will melt, leaving the herb ready to use. This method we have found very attractive for herbs for punch, small sprigs of mint for summer drinks, and sweet woodruff for May Wine. You can also freeze borage flowers, violas and tiny marigolds, which are more decorative than flavorful, with the ice cube method.

At Caprilands we freeze sorrel in large quantities for sorrel soup and bouillon. In our experience sorrel loses a little of its tangy sharp taste during processing. When substituting frozen sorrel for fresh in a recipe, it's best to use somewhat more than the fresh herb called for. Freeze sorrel leaves in plastic freezer bags. Sorrel and parsley resist the first fall frosts, so we have them both fresh from the garden until late November. Sorrel is the earliest of the vegetable herbs in spring, so at the worst we are only a short time without it. We use our frozen sorrel mainly in early April, before the new crop begins to come in.

Making Herbal Vinegars

Throughout the summer our visitors at Caprilands are intrigued by the appearance of gallons of what appears to be water, placed in the garden, among the plantings of basil, tarragon, mints, dill, burnet and chives. This is **not** water but white distilled vinegar waiting for the herbs to be placed in it as they mature and are ready for harvest. Some of the bottles have already been filled with the leaves and are waiting for the heat of the sun to cure and release the flavor into the liquid. In other places the presence of the unfilled jugs is a reminder that daily cutting must be done as soon as the herb matures.

The tops of the rapidly growing basil are cut frequently for if the top rosette of leaves is removed, the plant sets about growing a new crown of leaves immediately. It also grows new branches. This method of cutting back basil prevents the blossoms from forming, and the plant will continue to yield flavorsome leaves into the fall. Left to produce blossoms, it, being a true annual, has completed its life cycle and will start to yellow and toughen, producing smaller leaves and will often die. The harvested leaves are placed immediately in the vinegar until the bottle is three-quarters full. Then it receives three top cuttings of dark opal basil, for color, from a nearby bed. This will within two days tint the whole gallon a beautiful grenadine pink. Opal basil produces a lasting color even when it is exposed to the sun, unlike many other vegetable colors which fade in light. After a week in the sun the vinegar is ready to be stored in our cool cellar where it sets until the time to place it in individual bottles. It then comes to the kitchen where it is strained to remove old leaves and any sediment. We pour it through a funnel into smaller containers that may come directly to the table. We place a piece of fresh herb in each bottle. Basil, tarragon, thyme, and dill are all decorative and add extra fresh flavor to the final bottling. Sometimes we add cloves of garlic to the basil vinegar.

Heat from the sun releases the flavor of tarragon cuttings placed in jugs of distilled vinegar.

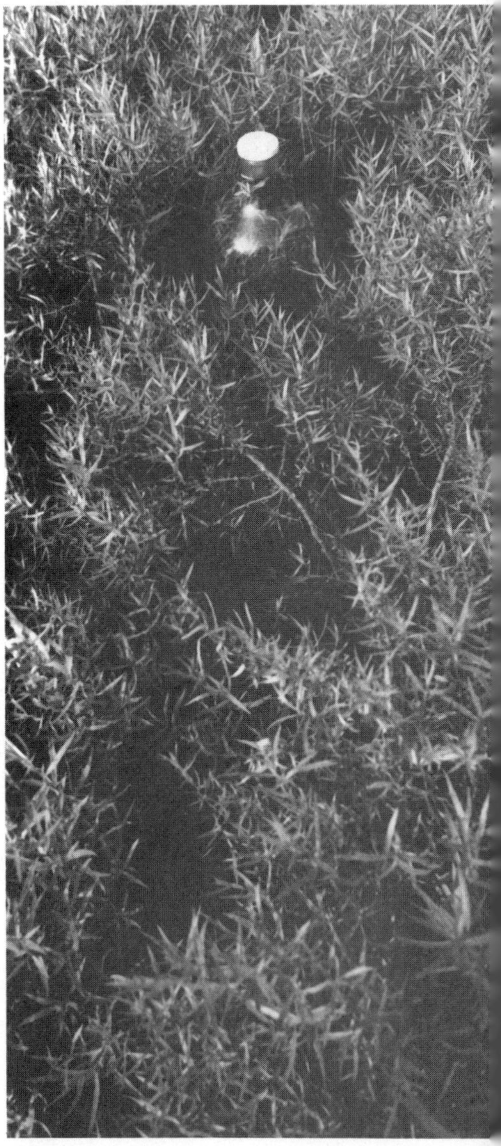

There are also spicy vinegars to be made. These are placed in beautiful old bottles, wine carafes, or hand blown glass from Spain, Italy and Mexico. For those who like a freshly-mixed dressing, done at the table, these handsome containers are most intriguing. Dill in a seagreen container is like an undersea picture, and the spicy basil, sports a long stick of cinnamon, peppercorns, allspice and peppers, both for taste and appearance.

Preserving Herbs in Cooking Oils

Preserving herbs in cooking oils provides cooks with excellent assistance in food preparation. A bland, flavorless oil is a good medium for herbal flavorings and is particularly recommended for those who are on a salt free diet. When the herbs are fresh, it takes about two weeks for them to permeate the oil with their essence; if they are dry, allow a longer time, another two weeks. This process may be hastened by heating the oil to the boiling point before pouring it over the herbs. It will then be a good marinade for meat, for some salads, or for frying.

Heads of dill maintain their shape in bottles of vinegar.

XVIII

Halloween Magic at Caprilands

At Caprilands we have a pleasant custom shared with many New Englanders. Through the year we decorate all our old doors with swags that have some meaning for the season. We struggle when we reach the harvest time for appropriate leaves and flowers, as there is such a wealth of materials that we hardly know what to choose. Nearly all the herbs are in some way protective, so there is a wide choice for our autumn doors. One of our most favored decorations is made of artemisia, with wormwood blossoms and a center of rowan berries surrounded with oak leaves. Tied with a brown and orange bow to which is added a sweet-toned bell that rings as people enter, it is a perfect protection from all "witchcraft."

If you wish to see witches at Halloween, there are several things which you may do according to ancient tradition. To ensure this special vision, bind together rue, agrimony, maiden hair, and ground ivy. This will, also, if placed by the doorway, "keep any witch who seeks to enter fastened on the threshold." Legend has it that if you use elder juice on your eyelids (the green juice of the inner bark), and if you are a baptized person, you will be able to see what the witches are about in any part of the world.

According to European folklore, strong smelling herbs such as hyssop, wormwood, mugwort and rosemary hung in the house would drive out infectious spirits. In the Orient, spices like sandalwood, cloves and musk were used for exorcism. Censing was employed to exorcise the evil spirits and to invoke the holy ones. Similar rituals persisted to our day in church ceremonies where incense is used to sanctify and to exorcise.

Here is a method from old Devonshire folklore to get rid of spells cast by wizards and witches: "Take certain medicines at certain stated times and a bundle of herbs. The paper of herbs is to be burnt, a small bit at a time, on a few coals with a little Bay and Rosemary, and, while it is burning, read the first two verses of the 68th psalm and say the Lord's Prayer after . . ."

To Make a Witch's Broom

The handle must be of ash. This will ensure the witch from ever getting her feet wet as she rides over large bodies of water. The sweeping part of the broom must be made of birch twigs which hold the evil spirits, so that no matter how much they cry they cannot escape. They assist in the witch's evil doing. The twigs are bound with osiers or willow twigs, for willow is the plant of sorrow. The handle

Witches on herbal brooms levitate in a shop window.

A witch with an herbal broom makes a Halloween decoration.

must be rubbed with Datura *(Datura stramonium),* wolfsbane, monkshood (*Aconitum* species), and moonwort (*Lunaria,* silver dollar) or magic fern, to give the rider levitation that he (or she) may rise off the ground. The useful besom, an important tool in so many European gardens, is sometimes called a witch's broom, and reversely, a besom may mean an old hag or witch.

The broom that witches ride has many uses. If laid across the threshold it will avert evil, if thrown after a bewitched cow or person it will protect them. At one time, if jumped over by a bridal couple, they were declared married. Flowering broom brought into the house in May presages death (in some English country places).

To Make a Witch's Wreath

Some essential plants to use in the composition of a magic wreath are rue, cranesbill blossoms (which is the wild geranium or herb Robert), willow for sorrow, hawthorn, elder, alder and the berries of the rowan tree. Dill, valerian, and vervain may also be added. Oak leaves may be a part of this magical group of herbs, too. In medieval times, the oak and the ash were used for and against witches, and were thought to either help or hinder the witch, depending upon their application.

Rowan sticks (mountain ash) were carried in the purses and pockets of many country people in England in the last century as a protection from evil spirits, and can be attached to the wreath. Holly may also be used for it is hated by witches. The holly's prickly leaves are reminiscent of the crown of thorns and the red berries of the blood of Christ falling to the ground, and therefore the plant came to be called Holy or Holly, and Christ Thorn. Bracken and ferns may also be used in the wreath and some branches of yew berries will add extra interest.

XIX

Cold Weather Salads

It is very easy to become attached to one type of salad and neglect the dozens of possibilities a good garden and well-stocked larder will provide. An herb garden, even a small one, will encourage experimentation, resulting in new tastes and excitements in presentation.

The green salad is so much a part of today's menu that we forget there was a time when winter greens were not available, and one had to resort to home-stored vegetables, canned fruits and greens for the cold days that followed late October frosts.

In the Vermont farmhouse where I spent part of my youth, the root cellar supplied winter vegetables. Our greens for the table were shredded cabbage, celery which had been preserved and blanched in sand, or canned garden greens, peas, beans, and jars upon jars of tomatoes. Added to this were squashes from the root cellar; hard winter hubbard were most highly prized. Then there were turnips, beets, and potatoes, white and sweet, all carefully stored. The cellarway smelled of apples, for we stored barrels of winter varieties, and in the kitchen, apples were drying on racks over the stove. Commercial canned goods in grocery stores hardly existed, and the few that appeared were highly suspect. We ate well with this cellar fare, but relished the green from the parsley plants that lived well in the cool pantry. But there are really a lot of salad ingredients available in the fall and winter if you use your imagination. There are even flowers still available for decorative salads.

September and October is flowering kale time. We grow this plant every year just for decoration, although it is good to eat in salads as well. Like all members of the cabbage family, it survives the frosts and is even better in cool weather. It grows a head that is shaped like a flower and may be green and white, or green and purple, or white tinged with purple and pink, always with some varigation. Kale is useable for some time if stored in the refrigerator. We once put it in a flower decoration on the table in water. In the heat of the room it soon disclosed its cabbage ancestry and gave off a strong and most unpleasant smell. But flowering kale is certainly the most effective salad decoration that the garden produces, well worth raising from seeds or purchased seedlings.

Late-flowering lilies can decorate cold weather salads.

Textured cabbage is a decorative ingredient in cold weather salads.

Recipes for Cold Weather Salads

Quick Beet Salad

- sour cream or yogurt
- chopped dill
- chopped chives
- 2 cups whole beets, cooked and chilled
- 2 cups chopped carrots
- 2 onions, thinly sliced
- greens

Make a dressing with the sour cream or yogurt and the dill and chives. Combine the beets, carrots, and onions with the dressing and arrange on the greens.
Serves 8 to 10.

Anise Pork and Apples

- 2 cups cubed roasted pork (rub pork with ground anise seed before roasting)
- 1 cup chopped celery
- ½ cup pecans or walnuts, chopped
- ½ cup salt-free relish
- 2 tablespoons chopped onion
- 1 cup mayonnaise
- ½ teaspoon mixed herb blend (Caprilands preferred or plain parsley)
- 2 tablespoons fresh lemon juice (½ lemon)
- 3 apples, cored and sliced

In a large bowl mix pork, celery, nuts, relish, and onion. Set aside. In another bowl mix mayonnaise with herb blend, or parsley. Add lemon juice. Toss with apples. Add mayonnaise mixture to pork mixture and combine well. Hint: To serve attractively, arrange pork and apple salad on greens with a red gelatin mold.
Serves 4 to 6.

Macaroni Salad

- ½ cup salad burnet, chopped
- 1 cup parsley, finely chopped
- ½ cup mayonnaise
- 3 cups elbow macaroni, cooked
- 2 cups chopped celery
- ¼ cups chopped green pepper
- ½ cup diced Provolone cheese
- kale and purple cabbage for garnish

Mix herbs with mayonnaise. Combine with rest of ingredients. Garnish bowl with kale and crisp purple cabbage.
Serves 6.

Tuna-Almond Salad

In a large bowl, combine lettuce, celery, apples, tuna, onions, and almonds. Whisk together mayonnaise and yogurt. Stir in herbs. Pour over tuna mixture and combine well.
Serves 6.

- 1 cup chopped lettuce
- 1 cup chopped celery
- 2 cups chopped apples
- 6½ ounces of tuna, water-packed
- 2 tablespoons finely chopped onions
- ¼ cup blanched almonds, slivered

- ½ cup mayonnaise
- ¼ cup yogurt
- 1 teaspoon mixed herbs

Sweet Potato Salad

In a large bowl, combine potatoes, celery, pineapple chunks, pork, nuts and sesame seeds. Whisk together ginger, mayonnaise, yogurt and marmalade. Pour dressing over potato mixture. Combine well.
Serves 8 to 10.

- 4 cups cubed cooked sweet potatoes
- 1 cup chopped celery
- 2 cups pineapple chunks
- 1 cup cubed cooked pork
- ¼ cup chopped nuts (walnuts, or pecans)
- ½ cup sesame seeds

- 1 teaspoon ground ginger
- ½ cup mayonnaise
- ½ cup plain yogurt
- ¼ cup orange marmalade

Coleslaw

Place chopped cabbage in a bowl of ice water. Refrigerate for 2 hours. Drain and put in a large bowl. Drain pineapple and add chunks to cabbage. Add oranges, apples, raisins, and onions and toss well.

Whisk mayonnaise, celery seed, pepper, and coriander together. Pour over cabbage mixture and combine well.
Serves 8 to 10.

- 1 medium head of cabbage, cored and chopped
- 15½ ounces pineapple chunks, chilled
- 2 naval oranges, peeled and quartered
- 1 apple, chopped
- ½ cup raisins
- 2 small onions, chopped

- 1 cup mayonnaise
- 1 tablespoon celery seed
- ¼ teaspoon black pepper, freshly ground
- 2 tablespoons ground coriander

Rowan tree berries turn brilliant red-orange in fall.

Autumn brings us the whole glowing harvest of the garden, in the reds of the zinnias, used only for effect, not for flavor, the flaming yellow and orange of marigolds, the red-orange rowan tree (mountain ash) berries, red barberries, purple grapes, and slices of squash. There are still lilies to be picked and, in the absence of other materials, the leaves of scented geraniums are tasty, sweet smelling, and good in the construction of a salad design.

Winter and Christmas should present a problem for cooks who want to make fanciful salads, but we have overcome the seasonal limitations. We bring some of our flowering plants into the greenhouse where the calendulas continue to blossom and the nasturtiums also strive for a while to present blooms. When they are gone we resort to the rosettes of canned artichoke hearts and sliced cucumbers placed in rhythmic patterns with black olives to make our geometric wonders. Cranberries and cut slices of oranges and lemons are also employed, the white of feta cheese, and the blue and white marbling of Roquefort help in taste and design.

In the herb garden, fennel stays green into December and is a feathery light garnish, very anise tasting. Sorrel also gives us its long, decorative sour leaves. Parsley is never better than at this time of year when we cut the large Italian type for its fern-like look and real distinctive flavor. Lovage has been cut many times, but is back again with a fine celery-like taste, and savoy cabbage, with its lovely crinkled edge, is useful both for meat and magic. We always cut some purple basil ahead of the killing frosts to enjoy its dark beauty and sweet odor all during the late summer and autumn. The last of the tarragon can now be used, as it will soon turn brown and the plant will go into its winter rest. Winter savory, however, stays green and makes thick mats, smelling very savory, like its name. Sprigs of thyme are used sparingly with the savory. Rosemary, of course, comes into its own now, its shining leaves giving off an odor of ginger and spice.

Under a fence rail potted mums add color through autumn days.

XX

Providing Winter Protection for Herbs

The gilliflower also, the skilfull do know,
doth look to be covered in frost and in snow:
The knot and the border, and rosemary gay,
do crave the like succour, for dying away.
—THOMAS TUSSER

One of the problems in the first years of herb gardening comes at the approach of fall. What to cut back, what to leave; what to mulch and what not to mulch; and what to bring into the house and what not to—these decisions have to be made every autumn. Fortunately, most herbs are hardy perennials that need no winter coddling. If you familiarize yourself with the plants you grow, determining whether each is an annual, biennial, perennial, or shrub, putting the herb garden to bed for the winter will be less puzzling and more an excuse to get outdoors and enjoy the brisk invigorating weather of the season.

To Cut or Not to Cut

Basically, plants in the herb garden are cut back after frost to make the garden neat. Certain perennials and most shrubs and trees are exceptions, because they will sprout again when the sap flows in spring. After an herb gardener harvests all summer and fall for winter arrangements and seasonings, many plants require little additional trimming.

These final cuttings end the year. The kitchen and the drying rooms should now be hung with the year's harvest. The days of winter cooking, teas by the fireside, and Christmas giving are happily stretched ahead.

Over our kitchen stove, that black iron relic of the past, which keeps the kitchen warm from mid October on through the winter, hang bunches of bright green parsley which dry quickly (overnight usually), and keep both their flavor and color. All across the ceiling on wires hangs our harvest of sage, to be, as soon as it is dried, transferred to plastic bags for those people who like their sage "in the leaf" for the Thanksgiving turkey.

The pleasant smell of woodsmoke becomes our autumn incense, the tea kettles hum and steam on the comfortable heat of the old stove while the kitchen dogs seek refuge under it. The shelves are bursting with old china and glass in forgotten patterns that are ever new and dear to me. There are special treasures for tea; now waiting for use are old fat teapots in country Staffordshire, satiny pewter or plain white farmhouse Ironstone. We are ready for the winter period to begin with the aroma of steaming herbal teas, and freshly baked breads.

Below, *foliage needs to be stripped from stems of flowers to promote effective drying.* Below right, *plants along roadsides and in fields can be gathered and dried with garden herbal material.*

Winter

Large groups frequently gather at Caprilands for instructions on making herb decorations. Here participants learn how to make an artemesia tree.

Many visitors to Caprilands during all of the seasons enjoy full-course meals.

The golden glow of straw and wooden ornaments compliments the red of the poinsettias.

Holiday cheer emanates into the night.

Red trinkets are especially effective on the silver branches of artemesia.

XXI

Winter Diary

A time to dream
A time to plan,
Time essential
To every man
—*A.G.S.*

The quiet aloneness of winter has a special charm for the herb gardener, and I confess this season is my delight. Through the restless, rushing hours of spring, and the long days of summer that begin at dawn and end with weeding in the twilight, I find myself looking back at the peace of the past winter, and forward to the next one. The winter landscape, bare and stringent, reveals a beauty of form and line that is not visible in spring and summer.

Through the small-paned windows of my northwest writing room, the winter landscape stretches toward the surrounding woodland. Here and there are patches of seed herbs, brown and disorderly, but food for birds in the cold days ahead. Clumps of perilla stand red-brown against the snow. They have furnished seeds for some time now, and the bird's appreciation of them has increased this plant's value to me so that I excuse its prolific growth. In the fields there are seeding southernwoods and oreganos with brown blossoms still fragrant. Some were forgotten, others were left as food for small wild animals.

XXII

Christmas at Caprilands

Now Christmas is come
Let's beat up the drum,
And call all our neighbors together,
And when they appear,
Let us make them such cheer
As will keep out the wind and the weather
—*WASHINGTON IRVING*

Caprilands is our home, a large, comfortable eighteenth-century farmhouse surrounded by fifty acres of fields and woods in Coventry in northern Connecticut. To the north, south, and west our boundaries are trees and meadows; to the east is the roadway, and we welcome our frequent visitors. In winter the strong lines of our colonial house, the sweep of the roofs, and balance in "ell" and outbuildings are seen against snow-covered fields and gardens. A few hemlocks close to the house break the austere lines and also offer protection to birds. We find all this an ideal setting for the festivities of the "long Christmas" we so enjoy.

But for the early New Englanders, Christmas was a day like any other. The twelve days so richly celebrated in the Old World brought stern disapproval from the Puritans. Many of today's traditions were considered heathen, as indeed they were, for pagan rituals from Greece and Rome, and rites of the Winter Solstice have merged for us with the

Feast of the Nativity and Epiphany, the coming of the Magi. Mistletoe, the "golden bough" of classical legend and sacred to the Druids, is still banned in churches, but candles and evergreen wreaths, once part of the ancient Saturnalia, are now acceptable in Christian ceremonies and have always been a part of our Christmas.

Christmas is the peak of the herb gardener's year, a time of long preparation, great anticipation, and much excitement. The dark days of Advent overflow with Christmas plans, and the best celebrations follow the true meaning of the season. They emphasize family traditions, but also borrow colorful customs from many lands and eras to weave a rich tapestry of prayers, parties, giving and receiving, dining and decorating.

Capriland buildings with small-paned windows create a traditional colonial farmhouse setting.

Recipes for the Holidays

Christmas Confetti Casserole

- 3 medium onions, sliced
- 1 cup celery, chopped
- ¼ pound butter
- 1 teaspoon basil
- ½ teaspoon dried marjoram or 1 teaspoon chopped fresh marjoram
- 1 cup parsley, chopped
- ½ teaspoon black pepper, freshly ground
- ½ cup pineapple chunks
- 4 pimientos, chopped
- 6 cups rice, cooked
- ½ cup blanched almonds, slivered

Prepare the sauce by cooking the onions and celery in the butter until soft. Add the basil, marjoram, half the parsley, and the pepper. Stir in the pineapple and pimientos. Pour the sauce over the rice, and fluff with a fork until the rice is well coated. Correct the seasoning as needed. Put in ovenproof casserole. Spread almonds over the rice, and sprinkle on the rest of the parsley. Hint: For an all-in-one-meal, add 2 cups chopped cooked chicken or tuna fish to the sauce. Add chives from the window box; dried parsley also may be used.) Bake in 350° oven 30–45 minutes until hot and bubbling.
Serves 8 to 12.

Curried Corn Soup

- ¼ pound butter
- 1 tablespoon curry powder
- 1 tablespoon powdered freeze-dry shallots
- 3 10-ounce packages frozen cream-style corn
- 2 10-ounce packages frozen corn
- 2 cups light cream, warmed
- ⅛ teaspoon ground rosemary or 2 sprigs chopped fresh rosemary
- 2 tablespoons chopped chives

Melt butter in pan, add curry, and stir until smooth. Add shallots and corn, stirring slowly; then cream and rosemary. Garnish with chives. (Evaporated milk or half-and-half may be substituted for medium cream.)
Serves 8.

Saffron Rice

- 1 cup brown rice
- 2 green peppers, seeded and chopped
- 1 cup chopped celery
- 2 onions, finely chopped
- 4 tablespoons butter
- 1 cup half and half or cream
- ½ teaspoon saffron threads
- 1 cup chicken stock
- 1 cup chopped cooked chicken
- parsley
- paprika

Preheat oven to 350°. Cook rice and set aside. In a 10-inch skillet, saute peppers, celery and onions in butter until soft. Soak saffron threads in chicken stock for 10 minutes. Add saffron plus stock and cooked chicken to skillet containing vegetables and combine. Place rice in a 2-quart ovenproof casserole. Add vegetable mixture to rice and mix well. Bake for 20 minutes.
Serve 6 to 8.

Caprilands Christmas Spread

In a medium saucepan, combine tomato puree or tomatoes, garlic, herbs and spices and mustard. Heat to a gentle boil over medium high heat. Reduce the heat slightly and simmer the mixture, uncovered, stirring occasionally, for about 15 minutes. If you used whole tomatoes, use a spoon to break them up as the mixture is cooking.

Reduce the heat to low and slowly add cheese, stirring constantly. Stir until cheese is melted, then remove from heat. To serve attractively, heat and serve on fingers of crisp toast, garnished with fresh basil from the window box or greenhouse.

Yields about 2½ cups.

- 2 cups tomato puree or 16 ounce can Italian-style tomatoes
- 2 cloves garlic, minced
- 1 teaspoon dried basil or 2 teaspoons chopped fresh basil
- ½ teaspoon dried oregano
- 2 sprigs fresh rosemary, chopped (about ½ teaspoon)
- dash of grated nutmeg
- 1 teaspoon fennel or caraway seeds
- ¼ teaspoon black pepper, freshly ground
- 2 tablespoons Dijon mustard
- ½ pound Monterey Jack cheese, grated

Saint Nicholas Red Fruit Punch

Combine the cider and juices with the fruits and taste for sweetness. Cranberry may seem tart to some children. Add honey if necessary. Pour juice mixture over a cake of ice in a punch bowl and spoon in hard-frozen sherbet. Garnish with fresh rosemary, and serve at once. Provide each person with a spoon for eating the fruit and sherbet.

Serves 30.

- 1 gallon sweet cider
- 1 gallon cranberry juice
- 1 quart orange juice
- 3 quarts mixed fresh fruit
- honey, optional
- 2 quarts homemade sherbet
- long rosemary sprigs

Christmas Potato Salad

Peel potatoes and cube. Chill thoroughly. Place cubed potatoes in a large bowl. Set aside. Chop 6 of the hard-cooked eggs, reserving the rest for garnish. Add chopped eggs and onions to potatoes and combine well.

In medium bowl combine mayonnaise with rest of ingredients. Pour mayonnaise dressing over potatoes. Chill.

Serves 12.

- 12 medium potatoes, boiled
- 12 hard-cooked eggs
- 1 large onion, finely chopped

- 2 cups mayonnaise
- 2 teaspoons mixed herbs
- 1 teaspoon dill seeds
- ½ clove garlic, crushed
- 2 teaspoons tarragon or garlic vinegar
- 2 tablespoons chopped salad burnet
- 1 small jar pimientos (reserve half for garnish)
- 12 to 15 salt-free pickles, chopped (optional)

Christmas Broccoli Mixture

- 4 10-ounce packages frozen broccoli, steamed
- ½ pound mushrooms, sliced
- 1 tablespoon butter
- 1 teaspoon chopped parsley

- ¼ pound butter
- ½ cup whole wheat flour
- 1 quart milk
- 2 cups shredded cheddar cheese
- black pepper to taste

- 3 tablespoons butter
- 2 large onions finely chopped
- 2 cups chopped cooked turkey or chicken
- ½ loaf whole grain bread, crumbled
- 1 tablespoon poultry seasoning
- 2 cups shredded cheddar cheese

Preheat oven to 350°. Place broccoli in a 4-quart ovenproof casserole that has been sprayed with a no-stick spray. Saute mushrooms in 1 tablespoon butter until wilted. Add parsley and combine with broccoli in casserole.

In a large saucepan, melt 1 stick butter over low heat. Add flour and whisk until a smooth paste is formed. Increase heat to medium and slowly add milk. Stir until sauce thickens. Stir in 2 cups shredded cheese. Continue heating until cheese melts. Season with pepper; remove from heat.

To prepare topping, melt 3 tablespoons butter in a large skillet. Saute onions until limp. Add cooked poultry, crumbled bread, and poultry seasoning. Combine well.

To assemble, pour cheese sauce over broccoli-mushroom mixture. Top with turkey-bread crumb mixture. Sprinkle with remaining cheese.

Bake at 350° for 55 minutes to one hour.

Serves 12.

Pain D'Èpice (Spice Bread)

- 1 teaspoon anise seed
- ¾ cup boiling water
- 1 cup dried fruit (Use a mixture of dried apricots, pears, dates and raisins, or whatever you have on hand.), chopped
- 1 cup honey
- 1½ cups whole wheat flour
- 1 cup unbleached white flour
- 1½ teaspoons baking soda
- 1 teaspoon cinnamon
- 1 teaspoon freshly grated nutmeg
- ½ teaspoon ground cloves

Preheat oven to 350°. Soak anise seed in boiling water for 5 minutes. Combine dried fruit and honey in a mixing bowl. While the anise mixture is still warm, stir into the honey mixture and mix well. Sift together the flours, baking soda and spices. Add dry ingredients to the honey mixture and stir until smooth. Pour the batter into a greased 9 × 5-inch loaf pan.

Bake at 350° for 45–50 minutes, or until a toothpick inserted in the loaf comes out clean. Immediately remove the loaf from pan and let cool completely on a wire rack. Wrap loaf tightly in plastic wrap and let stand one day before slicing. Slice bread very thin.

Yields 1 large loaf.

Caraway Cocktail Bread

In a large bowl, place oats, butter, honey, salt, raisins and caraway seeds. In a smaller bowl proof yeast with one cup of the lukewarm water. Pour the other cup of water over the mixture, let stand 15 minutes. Add yeast and water to oatmeal mixture. Stir in flours. Knead until smooth. Let rise in a warm place for 2 to 3 hours. Punch down and shape in 4 or 5 small loaves. Bake in a preheated 325° oven until done, about 45 minutes to an hour.
Yields 4 or 5 small loaves.

- 1 cup rolled oats
- 2 tablespoons butter
- ½ cup honey
- 1 teaspoon salt
- ½ cup muscat raisins
- 2 tablespoons caraway seeds
- 2 packages dry yeast
- 2 cups lukewarm water, divided
- 2½ cups unbleached white flour
- 2½ cups whole wheat flour

Anise Bread

Preheat oven to 350°. Mix flour with baking powder. Beat eggs with milk; gradually beat in honey. Combine flour mixture and egg mixture. Add melted butter. Beat for 3 minutes. Add anise seed or cardamom. Form into loaves in loaf pans and bake about 30 minutes in 350° oven.
Yields 2 loaves.

- 3 cups flour
- 4½ teaspoons baking powder
- 2 eggs
- 2 cups milk
- ¼ cup honey
- 2 tablespoons melted butter
- 5 teaspoons anise seed or 1 teaspoon cardamom seed

Cardamom Bread

Scald milk and cool to lukewarm. Combine warm milk with salt, honey, butter and yeast in a large mixing bowl. Let stand 5 minutes or until yeast is creamy. Using the tip of a paring knife, scrape seeds from the cardamom pods and grind with a mortar and pestle. Add cardamom and eggs to the yeast mixture and stir until blended. Add 4 cups unbleached white flour and 4 cups whole wheat flour and knead until smooth. (Add additional whole wheat flour if dough is sticky.)

Place dough in a greased bowl, cover and let rise in a warm place until doubled in bulk, 1½–2 hours. Punch down dough, divide in quarters, and let rest 5 minutes. Form into four long loaves and place on greased cookie sheets. Cover and let rise in a warm place about 30 minutes. About 15 minutes before the bread is finished rising, preheat the oven to 325°. Bake bread at 325° for 30 minutes or until done. Remove from pan and cool.
Yields 4 large loaves.

- 2 cups milk
- 1 teaspoon salt
- ½ cup honey
- 4 tablespoons butter
- 2 packages dry yeast
- 10 cardamon pods (or 1 teaspoon ground cardamom)
- 4 eggs, lightly beaten
- 4 cups unbleached white flour
- 4–4½ cups whole wheat flour

The herb gardener has a wealth of materials to put to use in holiday celebrations—decorative aids from the garden and dried seasonings for cooking. This is the time to use your herb garden; to make the personal gifts that money cannot buy; to serve the foods of many lands made exceptional by herbs; a time to use the spices symbolic of the Wise Men; to serve the wassails of Merrie England and the lands of the far North.

The Christmas season ushers in the happiest and busiest time of my year. The house is filled with the color and sweet odor of evergreens that adorn every corner and frame the long living room where our activities take place. Greens are of many varities, and all have herbal histories and uses, from the tall pyramidal junipers in the four corners of the room, to the bits of pennyroyal in the manger bed of the Christ Child in our creche.

In a large window that looks across the fields, great rosemary shrubs with shining needle leaves make a fragrant silhouette against a snow white or bleak brown world. Theirs is the true scent of Christmas, spicy with a hint of ginger, that permeates the room as the sun strikes the leaves or we brush them in passing.

Juniper, from nearby pastures and overgrown farmlands, with its frosty resinous berries and silver-backed branches; cedars, thick-branched and yellow-green; long-needled pine; and the satiny luxuriant yew, elegant, dark, and mysterious—all these evergreens make the frame on which our Christmas decorations are built, and provide the background for a joyous season.

We enjoy treks to the grove which has furnished us with our greens for the past few years. It is a sheltered place, a natural bird sanctuary, on a sloping hillside, filled with light and sun. The thick cedars grow there as though planted by some celestial landscape artist, or a Druid priest transported from the old world past to recreate an enchanted wood and a new world. Pillar-like these tall trees are, with the branches reaching up, growing thick, and close to the slim strong trunks. Blue berries are the fruits, in some years most abundant and very decorative. Their seed furnishes a potent source for new trees, and there are always many small young seedlings growing beside the parent trees.

The variety of herbal gifts is limitless.

XXIII

Wreaths from the Herb Garden

Joan can call by name her cows,
And deck her windows with green boughs;
She can wreathes and tutties make,
And trim with plums a bridal cake.
—THOMAS CAMPION

In the last days of November, when it would be pleasanter perhaps to stay by the fire, I start down the hillside with a basket to fill with herbs for making wreaths—part of the garden's contribution to Christmas decoration. Any garden that has santolina, germander, horehound, rue, lamb's-ear, lavender, sage, winter savory, and thyme provides a wealth of material for holiday cutting. I take rosemary from the greenhouse where it winters in large terra-cotta tubs and bushel-baskets. All this fragrant material stands in water, in a larger copper bowl, until I can use it.

The History of Wreath Making

The making of wreaths is an ancient and honored art that began about a thousand years before the birth of Christ. A crown of oak leaves adorned the warrior, ivy rewarded the poet, and statesmen were dignified under their laurels. Laymen did not wear these crowns, only men of distinction. Roman generals were crowned as they returned from war with wreaths made of grass and wild flowers from the battlefields.

At Christmas the wreath is symbolic of Christian immortality. The circle and the sphere are symbols of immortality. Traditionally, the wreath has been worn at festivals, at sacrifices, at weddings, and banquets. The priests wore henbane, vervain, and rue, plants long associated with the other world and religious rites. Crowns for victors were made of laurel *(Laurus nobilis),* oak, olive, parsley, palm, and poplar. Brides wore coronets of orange blossoms, myrtle, or rosemary. Funeral wreaths were made of daffodils, poppies, and other plants that meant remembrance or everlasting life, as amaranth, statice, tansy and yarrow.

Sage adds fragrance to herb wreaths, in addition to texture.

Thyme may be used in green or dried form during the holidays.

As an everlasting, tansy has always symbolized lasting life.

How to Make a Living Wreath

Start with a hollow circle planting-form about 12 inches across and fill it with moist, unmilled sphagnum moss. Place this on a black or dark green metal tray, or on an old pewter plate. Insert cuttings of green santolina thickly all the way around the circle so as to cover the brown moss. All this forms the base of the wreath and stays fresh and green indefinitely. Next make an inside edge of gray *Santolina chamaecyparissus,* and repeat on the outer edge. Then group lavender and a rosette of lamb's-ears on one side, spreading out the leaves to make a flower-like shape. On the opposite side, insert a rosette of young horehound plants.

The tops of clary sage and seasoning sage make decorative accents when used at intervals around a wreath. The deep purple-gray of *Salvia officinalis* Purpurascens and the variegated foliage of Tricolor sage are also interesting additions. Insert sprigs of silver and gold thyme for a different leaf form and the lemon aroma. Continue the wreath by inserting stiff silvery cuttings of the gray, narrowleaf French thyme. The blue-green tops of rue make fine accents around the wreath. At this point, I often put a design of rosemary at the base of the wreath; if it is a perfect circle I make two designs, one for the top and one for the bottom.

The secret of success with this wreath design is to keep the outer edge a solid line of gray or green with one kind of plant for this basic line. Hold contrasting material generally to the center, and do not place large leaves so that they break the neat outline of the circle. If you do not have enough green santolina, use substitutes, as small-leaved English ivy, periwinkle *(Vinca minor),* or myrtle *(Myrtus communis),* sweet woodruff, and *Euonymus japonicus* var. *microphyllus.*

To keep the wreath fresh, provide plenty of moisture and light, but no hot sun. My wreaths stay healthy and even form roots in a west window where there is good light all day but no sun. The living wreath will fare better if it is in a cool place at night. If, despite all precautions, some materials dry, the wreath can still be made attractive by adding other dried herbs.

You can make this wreath into a hanging door decoration by lacing the frame lightly with florists wire. Carefully cover the back of the wreath with heavy aluminum foil so that moisture will not mar your door. Tie on a moss-green and white bow, add bayberries, and attach the wreath, firmly, top and bottom, to the door.

The Advent Wreath

Thanksgiving week is the time to gather materials for the Advent wreath made of herbs associated with the Holy Family. I use Savin juniper, rosemary, Our Lady's bedstraw, thyme, pennyroyal, rue, lavender, horehound, sage, true myrtle *(Myrtus communis)* and the purple, white, and pink flowers of dried globe amaranth *(Gomphrena globosa)*. Mechanics are the same as for the living wreath.

Cover the moist sphagnum moss with clippings of Savin juniper inserted thickly and deeply right into the wire frame. Press four pieces of floral clay, each large enough to hold the base of a 12-inch candle, and place these clay holders equidistant around the wreath. Complete the wreath with other herbal materials and small bows of purple velvet, changing these to pink for the third Sunday.

Traditionally, the Advent wreath was hung, but today the table wreath is usually preferred because it serves as centerpiece for the dinner table, and the candles may be watched during the meals. The German custom was to light a candle each Sunday of Advent, and for the family to read and memorize scriptures from the Old and New Testaments. At the end of Advent all candles were lighted, the final verses read and the celebration of Christmas begun.

An Everlasting Wreath of Artemisia

The form for this wreath is a circle to represent eternity and the projection of this world into the next. The herbal flowers symbolize immortality, with golden blossoms signifying the gifts of the Magi and also representing the light of the world. This artemisia wreath is made to last, not just for one year but for several.

Basic materials include an abundance of artemisia stalks (preferably those fresh from the garden), two dozen or more dried or freshly cut tansy blossoms, dried yarrow flowers, oregano blossoms (dried for deep browns, and fresh flowers which will dry first to purple or green), everlastings (preferably the roadside gnaphalium, dried, then shaken outdoors to remove the fluff), seed pods of rue, ambrosia, and the dried brown tips of St. John's-wort. You may also experiment with other materials such as sumac berries and various pine cones. Before starting to make the wreath, have at hand a roll of florists wire, sharp clippers to cut it, and a circle of heavy wire from 8 to 12 inches in diameter.

Arrange the artemisia stalks thickly and evenly around the circle of wire. Let stems overlap and press them down then bind them lightly into place with florist wire, leaving 1 to 2 inches between the strands as you wrap it around the wreath. Flatten the artemisia with both hands, adding more wire if necessary. This forms the base on which to place your best cuttings. (You may want to prepare several artemisia foundations at one time, then decorate them at others. We frequently make up bases a year in advance, using artemisia that has not yet headed since it will be concealed by full plumes from the new crop.)

Take your whitest artemisia (if you want a brown effect, use plants harvested later), remove the curls or stems from the treelike blossoms,

To begin an artemesia wreath arrange the stalks thickly and evenly around a wire circle.

Insert short full stems in the base.

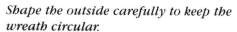

Shape the outside carefully to keep the wreath circular.

When the wreath is nicely rounded, add decorations.

or cut the tops from the wispy ones that have not properly developed, and cut with stems long enough to insert in the base. Turn the curls toward the center, working clockwise until the circle is filled. Shape the outside line carefully as you work to keep a good circle. If the material is unruly, run a wire lightly around the whole wreath, lacing in the errant pieces, then cover the wire with more artemisia sprays. Save some of the laciest pieces for the center. Push these firmly into the framework, being careful to maintain a circle.

The wreath is now ready for floral decoration. Add a circle of tansy, then use yarrow toward the bottom. Make a circle of the everlastings, pressing their soft stems among the sturdier ones already in the wreath. Follow these with a ring of oregano, then ambrosia on the inside of the circle or pushed into the design for a green, mossy effect. Use the St. John's-wort and rue pods as pins and add small sprigs of dried lanceleaf goldenrod to give the design liveliness.

When the flowers are all placed, reshape the artemisia and add small curving pieces. Bows of yellow and brown velvet with a group of small cones or a rosette of tiny brass bells complete the festive appearance of this everlasting wreath. It may be used inside or in a sheltered doorway where wind and rain will not harm it. When not in use, wrap carefully in polyethylene film and store in a safe place. Restoration the second and following seasons is a simple matter of showering the wreath briefly under a spray faucet (remove the velvet bows first), hanging it to dry in a warm place, and then adding some of the current season's artemisia and herbal flowers.

Fragrant Wreath of Flowering Herbs

A wreath to be decorated with dried flowers, seed pods, and cones requires a full, lacy base, and more artemisia is needed than for the kitchen wreath. Follow the directions given above for making the artemisia base but use more of the showy white curls throughout. Before decorating, hang up the wreath to check its shape from every angle and to add more artemisia if necessary.

The bow is the only part of the wreath that must be removed when a wreath is freshened with a spray of water.

If you gather blossoms of the same herb at different times, you will have many delicate shades to work with. I often select materials in whites, browns, and grays, using pale yellows for accent, as everlastings, brown oregano, and the last blossoms of tansy. Some of the other herbs I use are golden yarrow, white yarrow, goldenrod, statice and ambrosia. Be wary of strawflowers. Their intense colors may overpower the muted tones of your herbal flowers. The tiny home-grown type can be effective, however. It helps to lay materials on top of the artemisia to develop the complete design before weaving them permanently into the base.

An Herb and Spice Wreath

This fragrant and attractive circle of spices and herbs makes a perfect decoration for the kitchen. Use the artemisia base, adding a circle of bay leaves with the lower edge left open. Point the bay leaves toward the center of the circle. In the lower edge arrange one of two nutmegs. Group three cinnamon sticks and wire them into the nutmeg, then add cardamom in the same cluster. The finishing touch consists of sprigs of rosemary inserted all around the outside of the wreath for a green frame. If you make this wreath as a gift, add two or three clear cellophane bags of seed herbs, such as coriander, caraway and anise. Make a bow of brown or moss-green velvet ribbon and with it secure the seed packets to the wreath.

In making an herb and spice wreath, you may wish to add whole, dried ginger root, whole mace, groups of sage leaves, or sprigs of thyme and savory, both winter and summer types.

An herb and spice wreath makes an attractive kitchen decoration.

XXIV

Christmas Traditions

Each year at Caprilands we try to lengthen the Christmas season. It is such a happy time of year. We now begin Christmas and decorations with St. Martin's Day (November 11) and continue on with St. Barbara's Day (December 3), St. Nicholas Day (December 6) and St. Lucy's Day (December 15). We use one of the earliest of the European celebrations for our inspiration—St. Nicholas Day.

St. Nicholas was a rich and famous bishop in the early days of the Christian church, and became one of the most loved saints of all time. As patron saint of children, especially school boys, of poor maidens, of sailors, of travelers and merchants, as a protector against thieves and robbers, as chief patron saint of Russia and seaport towns of Italy, his name was constantly used in prayers of Christian people.

For his many generous acts he was called the saint of the people, although he gave his name to czars of Russia, and was invoked by the peaceable citizen, the laborer, and the merchant.

Nicholas was born in Panthere, a city in Lycia, Asia Minor. His parents were Christians of illustrous birth and great wealth. He was a most extraordinary child, virtuous from birth and so unusually religious that his parents dedicated him at an early age to the church.

Soon after his ordination as a priest, his father and mother died of a plague and left him their vast fortune, which he immediately started to use in charitable works. It is as a giver of gifts that St. Nicholas is best remembered especially at Christmas time.

One of the most picturesque incidents connected with this benevolent saint occurred while he was still a young man. In his city there lived a nobleman and his three daughters who through a turn of

Wreaths are displayed with statues in shop.

fortune had become impoverished. Their lives consisted of miserable days of starvation without hope. Although the nobleman wished to arrange marriages for his daughters, this was impossible for he was too penniless to provide a dowry for them.

After much deliberation, his only recourse seemed to be to sell them into slavery. The knight was most reluctant to make this desperate move and put off the dreaded day as long as possible.

One night as the daughters were weeping in their chambers, hungry, cold and helpless, a bag of gold suddenly came through the casement window. Great was their joy and surprise as this furnished the necessary dowry for one of the sisters. Shortly after this miracle, or so it seemed, a second and a third bag of gold appeared in the same manner. On the last occasion the grateful father was watching. He caught the dignified Bishop by the hem of his robe and knelt before him filling the air with his cries of gratitude.

Nicholas waved him away and begged him to keep the visits a secret saying that great fortunes were given by God to share with others less fortunate.

For many years the secret of the bags of gold was secure, but at last became known, for the Bishop had become a familiar figure as he rode about the countryside on his great white horse distributing gifts. St. Nicholas in his role as Patron Saint of Mariners came to be especially revered in Holland. Here he was always represented as the richly dressed bishop in full ecclesiastical regalia.

He rode tall and straight on his white horse carrying bags of gold as gifts for the deserving, while behind him trudged his servant Black Peter, laden with switches for the children who misbehaved.

Because this venerable man loved children and his early life gave many examples of his protection of them, he came to be known as the distributor of gifts in the low countries.

On December 6th (St. Nicholas Day) or December 5th (St. Nicholas Eve), children placed wooden shoes on the doorsteps in the hope that the good Bishop would reward them with the traditional gifts of chocolate, other sweets or even a gold piece.

In recent ceremonies, in one of the ports of Holland a ship comes in bringing the St. Nicholas in full regalia. He is driven with great pomp to the city hall where he speaks to the people praising them for the good that they have done and reprimanding them for their errors.

After the ceremony there is special holiday fare to be tasted and a real celebration follows. Christmas comes later as a religious holiday, a true Holy Day, and is not confused with gift giving.

At Caprilands, we continue our Christmas celebrations for over a month after starting on December 6th. We are always reluctant to take down the greens and glitter after we celebrate the Feast of Lights and the coming of the Magi on January 6, Twelfth Night.

Wheat weaving produces traditional decorations for some trees in the Caprilands rooms.

XXV

The Scented Geraniums

As aromatic plants bestow
No spicy fragrance while they grow,
But crush'd or trodden to the ground,
Diffuse their balmy sweets around.
—*OLIVER GOLDSMITH*

The sweet-leaved geraniums can be enjoyed in winter and have a nostalgic charm. The scent of just one crushed lacy leaf of rose geranium brings back the past—tall Victorian houses with dormer windows, cupolas, porches like valentines, and big bay windows filled with plants. And these windows were cool and sunny. Fires banked at night did not radiate much heat, and in cold weather plants were protected from freezing by layers of newspaper slipped between them and the windows.

It was in this environment that the rose geranium grew to an astonishing size and provided slips for neighbors and friends as well as leaves for jelly and a sweet odor for the hands of visiting children. Other geraniums—the peppermint and the oakleaf—trailed over the sills, and the Apple and Nutmeg had green and gray masses of small leaves that were like bits of velvet in the sun. The lemon geranium grew so large that it looked like an exotic tree, with its tightly curled leaves growing in rings around the stalks. It was often set on the floor, planted in a butter tub. When you brushed against a plant, the lemon odor came so clean and fresh that you always went back again just to touch the vigorous, crisp leaf and to draw a long breath.

Children like to hear how, in the early days of the seventeenth century, the Dutch and English sailing ships brought the first sweet-smelling geraniums home from long voyages to the South African Cape. Sailors then, as now, looked for some gift to carry to those awaiting their return, and they found the geranium part of the strange world before Europe.

It was about 1632 that the first scented geraniums arrived in Europe. Interest in the plants spread quickly, and at the end of the century they had attained much favor. By 1750 colonial America and the geranium had met, and by 1870 the plant gained such popularity that over one hundred fifty varieties were listed in catalogs. This is the period most remembered for windows full of geraniums. They had now become readily available, and even those who lived in remote farm-houses had access to several kinds.

The tall narrow windows at Caprilands are an ideal place to grow scented geraniums.

Geranium or *Pelargonium*

While the scented geraniums are members of the vast geranium family, they are classified botanically as species and varieties of the genus *Pelargonium.* All of the geraniums commonly cultivated as pot plants—the zonals, Martha Washingtons, and scenteds—are in reality pelargoniums that came originally from the South African Cape. There they are just perennials that grow into sizable shrubs and trees, just as they do in southern California.

Scented geraniums are not only nostalgic reminders of old gardens, plant windows, and grandmother's kitchen, but they are attractive enough to create interest even without their pleasant associations. Leaf forms may be laced, fanshaped, divided like a pheasant's foot, a crow's foot, an oak leaf, a maple leaf, a ruffle, a crisp ruff, a grape leaf, or a

Some of the scented geraniums have especially lacey leaves.

spreading umbrella. Texture may be velvety or sticky.

The scents in many varieties are as strong as those of the fruits and flowers from which they derive their names. 'Rober's Lemon Rose' holds its scent longer than the rose, and the peppermint geranium *(P. tomentosum)* fairly makes your mouth water. One of the lemon geraniums *(P. crispum)* is so truly citrus-like that it suggests a refreshing glass of lemonade on a hot summer day.

The scented geraniums give off a pleasing odor when they are brushed, and yield a fragrant oil which may be distilled. The fragrance comes from the back of the leaves, and it is released by stroking or brushing them. Our grandmothers soaked the leaves in vinegar or alcohol to make sweet waters to bathe an aching head. The French, however, in their search for new sources of essences for perfumes discovered, about 1800, that *P. capitatum, P. roseum* and *P. odoratissimum* could substitute for the rare and extravagantly expensive attar of roses. From that time on, fields of the scented geraniums were grown in North Africa and southern France for distillation. About one pound of leaves is required to produce one gram of oil. Three ounces of oil is dissolved in a gallon of alcohol to make the sweet extract with a real rose odor that is one of the principal oils used in soap and potpourri and perfume.

The sweet-scented geraniums can be planted in the garden when the danger of frost is past.

XXVI

Winter Tea Party

The Muse's friend, tea does our fancy aid,
Repress those vapours which the head invade,
And keep that palace of the soul serene.
—*EDMUND WALLER*

In midwinter with the garden at rest and spring planting too far away to worry about, I turn my energy to the greenhouse and writing table, with time left each day to sip a cup of fragrant tea. Tea-drinking was the favorite social pastime of the American colonists. We all recall the story of the Boston Tea Party, and "Liberty Tea." With the tax on tea representing injustice, patriotic ladies banished real tea from their tables and turned to other leaves for a satisfying beverage.

The housewife as well as the lady of fashion tried mints, sages, balms, rosemary, camomile, and many others, both for medicinal value and flavor. Many of these teas proved unpalatable, but some pleasant combinations have remained with us. The name, "Liberty Tea," suggests to me a group of women gathered in a drawing room with thin china cups ready to receive the latest herbal brew; or two farm wives heating the copper kettle over the fire on a stormy afternoon while they gossip and exchange recipes and remedies. For these gatherings, teas were often sweetened with wild honey and sometimes made more palatable by the addition of homemade wine or brandy. As China tea returned to use, most of the herb teas were relegated to the health department, only a few were still appreciated for flavor.

At Caprilands we sometimes have a tea-tasting party when all the teapots are brought out, each one containing a different herbal brew. Guests are given a small pouring of each kind, with teacakes, breads, and cookies for balance. Years ago at our first sitting of this kind, I served twelve teas, too many for proper tasting, and everyone grew drowsy. Some dropped off completely. The effect was that of an opium party. In those far-off days my guests assisted in the dishwashing, but it was with great difficulty that I got help with my twelve teapots and the cups. I learned that day to use herbs with more caution.

An arrangement of dried flowers serves as a reminder of the glories of summer on a sunny winter day.

When to Serve Tea

The tea ceremony is a ritual not only for the Oriental and the English, but for herb gardeners and their fortunate friends the world over. The connoisseur of tea finds the garden, the woods and fields filled with leaves and blossoms to lend their essences to fine brews. To the confirmed tea drinker, almost any time is tea time, but for many of us there is a special hour that seems just right for this indulgence. Some have their hour on the terrace in the shadows and coolness of the late afternoon. Others have a cup ready on the kitchen table to sip during a busy day. Many of us remember special times when, in a shadowy old house on a wet spring day, with the garden practically swimming, we have spent a pleasant hour drinking tea from old brown Staffordshire.

Here at Caprilands, herb tea will always be associated with winter sunsets. This is the time in the short winter day when the pink light of late afternoon colors the snowy fields, and darkness creeping from the shadow of the woods dims the view from my windows. There is a chill on this hour of sunset and a sense of melancholy. This is the hour to bring in firewood for the night, and as I visit the woodshed, passing by the baskets of sweet smelling herbs, they give off their odors graciously as I brush by them.

Generous bunches of herbs attractively displayed add a feeling of comfort to a household in wintertime.

Recipes for a Winter Tea Party and Scented Geranium Treats

Calendula Tea

I use this herb, with mints, in making a mint tea. In the past it was used as an aid to complexion beauty, and it is said to be healing to the heart and good for the spirit. *Calendula officinalis* is a small-flowered, Mediterranean plant from which the large-flowered garden hybrids came. Both make a good tea and add bright color to herbal mixtures. I dry calendula blossoms all through the summer and even into late fall, for they often bloom after frost has killed every other flower. I store the dried petals in airtight jars and have them ready to use in tea mixtures at the rate of ½ teaspoonful per cup.

Camomile Tea

The mature flowers of two plants, *Chrysanthemum parthenium* and *Anthemis nobilis,* are harvested for this. The petals disappear when dry and only the yellow seed heads remain. They yield a slightly bitter brew that is refreshing for headaches and nausea, good for the nerves, and soporific. This is a household medicine and one of the most popular drinks in Europe. Allow a heaping teaspoonful of the seed heads to a cup of water; brew in a teapot. Strain before serving.

Caprilands Tea

Remembering the many virtues that herbs have and could contribute to our well being, I have mixed a tea of rich symbolism. If you drink it, theoretically you should enjoy these benefits: wisdom from mint, memory from rosemary, immortality and domestic happiness from sage, bravery from thyme, happiness from marjoram, a good complexion and a bright outlook on life from calendula, and soothed nerves and a good night's sleep from camomile. Furthermore, this tea tastes good. To make it, mix equal parts of the dried herbs and allow 1 heaping teaspoonful to 1 cup of boiling water.

Mint Teas

Mint is the herb most associated with teas. *Mentha piperita* is the strongest of the flavors and in its own right without other herbs, makes a good drink for those who wish to replace China tea or coffee as a beverage. Peppermint was used medicinally for heat prostration and to avert or cure nausea. I associate my first real experience with peppermint tea with a visit to a garden called "Deo Gratias." A lovely, restful place constructed on different levels, it gave the appearance of great size, although, actually it occupied only the area of an average backyard. It should have been a place to enjoy, but my companion was suffering from a severe headache that spoiled her pleasure in the garden. She was urged to rest on a comfortable garden seat with the green "nave" of the church garden stretching before her. Soon a pot of steaming hot peppermint tea was brought to her, and never was it more appreciated. The headache disappeared and the world came into focus again.

Although I had often served herb teas before this episode, I had not fully believed in them. From that time on I have felt greater confidence in urging people to drink them. Apple mint is so prolific I feel it cries to be used for good purpose. Now we cut it about three times in the season for a magnificent harvest. We store the leaves in airtight cans and in the winter use them in a mixed herb tea with this mint for a base.

Lemon Balm Tea

Pour 1 pint of boiling water over 1 ounce of the leaves, dry or preferably green. Let this steep for 10 minutes. Strain. Sweeten with honey. Recommended for feverish colds.

Rose Geranium Pudding Cake

Preheat oven to 300° and lightly grease a 1½-quart ovenproof casserole and arrange the rose geranium leaves on the bottom.

Beat together egg yolks, lemon rind and honey until thick and lemon-colored. Add lemon juice, flour and milk and beat until combined. In a separate bowl, beat egg whites until stiff but not dry. Fold egg whites into batter, and pour into prepared casserole. Place casserole in a large baking pan and pour water into the pan to come halfway up the sides of the casserole. Bake at 300° for 1 hour. Remove from oven and invert immediately onto a large plate with a lip.
Serves 6–8.

- 4 rose geranium leaves
- 3 eggs, separated
- 2 teaspoons grated lemon rind
- ½ cup honey
- ¼ cup lemon juice
- 3 tablespoons whole wheat pastry flour
- 1 cup milk

Rose Geranium Tea Biscuits

Dissolve yeast in ¼ cup lukewarm water to which has been added ¼ cup honey. Beat eggs with salt and add. In another bowl mix 1 tablespoon shortening, 1 tablespoon of warm water, and scalded milk. Let cool, then pour into the yeast-and-egg mixture. Add 5 to 5½ cups of flour. Mix well.

Put in a pan and let rise in a warm place until double in bulk. Combine rose geranium leaves, honey, butter, orange rind and flour. Divide dough in half, roll out like jelly roll and spread with rose geranium mixture. Roll up and slice into 1-inch pieces.

Arrange on waxed paper in a pan. Again, let rise until double in bulk and bake in a preheated 400° oven for about 30 minutes.
Yields 48 biscuits.

- 1 package dry yeast
- ¼ cup lukewarm water
- ¼ cup honey
- 2 eggs
- 1 teaspoon salt
- 1 tablespoon shortening
- 1 tablespoon warm water
- 1 cup milk, scalded
- 5–5½ cups flour
- 6 large finely chopped rose geranium leaves
- ½ cup honey
- ½ cup melted butter
- grated rind of 1 orange
- 1 teaspoon lemon juice
- 2 tablespoons flour

XXVII

A Time to Plan

Winter is the time to enjoy the planning of an herb garden, and these plans become increasingly ambitious with the reading of books, magazines, and catalogs. As the snows melt and the first balmy days of spring draw the gardener out of doors, the task ahead is brought nearer. Obstacles unseen, or brushed aside in the fine enthusiasm of developing a perfect design on paper, suddenly become realities. Often the plan must be revised quickly to make it practical. But all is done with optimism, and the basic winter planning proves worthwhile.

Whether the herb garden is small or large, it needs to be exquisitely neat and weedless, with wide paths and compact borders, the same plant often repeated to make a good showing. A background is important, a hedge, wooden fence, or stone wall, perhaps with espaliered trees. For new gardens by modern houses a fence of cedar, redwood, or grape stake looks well. Here at Caprilands, I wanted a fence in keeping with our eighteenth-century Connecticut farmhouse, so I built a three-board fence of weathered gray chestnut. This encloses some of the garden areas, and also furnishes support for taller plants and vines.

Your herb garden is not complete until there is a place for you to sit comfortably with room for a companion or so. I like benches of well-weathered wood best. Antique washbenches can sometimes be found and they are in keeping with most herb gardens. Iron furniture, painted black or dark green, is practical and not too blatant, but wood really looks better. If your benches and other furniture look handmade, they will appear as a natural part of the garden.

A good plan is all important for a garden that is full of delights. Certainly the most difficult garden is the one that is unplanned. The most delightful way to spend the last few weeks of winter is in contemplation and planning of the next season's herb garden.

And all without were walkes and alleys dight
With divers trees enranged in even rankes
And here and there were pleasant arbours pight
And shadie seats, and sundry flowering bankes
To sit and rest the walkers' weary shankes.

—*Edmund Spenser*

Winter is a time to dream about new garden paths and ornaments that will add a touch of whimsy.

A garden gate is an interesting backdrop for plantings.

Glossary of Herbs

Aconite
Ranunculaceae

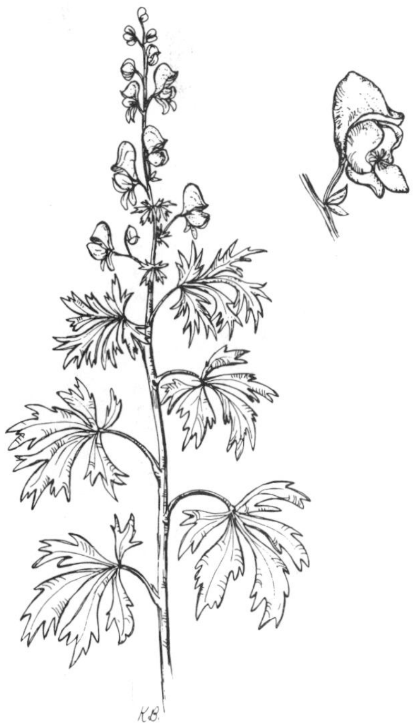

Aconite

The root of aconite *(Aconitum napellus)* has long been known as a source of poison once used on arrows to destroy wolves, hence the name "wolfbane." In the middle ages, this plant was known as monkshood or helmet flower, owing to the shape of the flower.

Description:
Hardy perennial, to 4 feet. Leaves divided two or three times into narrow segments. Flowers in blue or purple spikes. Old roots last only a year and new plants are produced by young shoots from the parent.

Uses:
Very decorative for late summer and fall color, but dangerous to have around children. Medicinally it should be used only by a physician.

Culture:
Partial shade with evenly moist, rich soil. Propagate by division of the roots in autumn. Spring-sown seeds reach maturity in two or three years.

Agrimony

Rosaceae

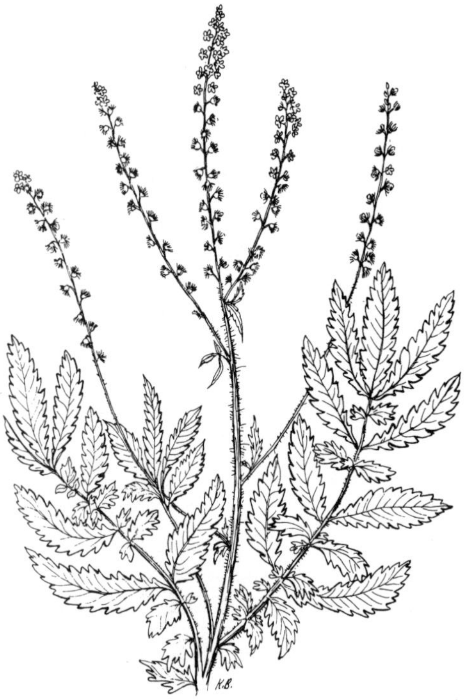

Agrimony

Common agrimony *(Agrimonia eupatoria),* also known as church steeples and cocklebur, received its generic name from the Greek word *argemone,* applied to plants that were healing to the eyes. The specific name *eupatoria* refers to Mithridates Eupator, a famous king who concocted remedies. Agrimony was once used for jaundice and skin disorders, and with mugwort and vinegar as a back rub. It is still collected as a medicinal herb in England.

Description:

Hardy perennial, 1 to 3 feet. Leaves similar to those of a wild rose. Flowers yellow, small, and numerous, occurring close together on a slender spike from June to September. The plant is downy and gives off a pleasant odor. It grows wild in Scotland.

Uses:

The whole plant, dried and ground, can be made into a tea said to be an excellent spring tonic. Historically, the yellow blossoms served as a source of dye.

Culture:

Dry soil with full sun or light shade. Propagate by sowing seeds collected from a dried spike. Germinates easily and, once established, it self-sows.

Ambrosia

Chenopodiaceae

Ambrosia

Ambrosia *(Chenopodium botrys)* is known also as Jerusalem oak and father geranium.

Description:

Hardy annual, 2 feet, decorative and fragrant. Self-sown seedlings appear in May with leaves like those of a small oak tree. They are red on the back, dark green and marked like an oak on the top. As the plant grows, feathery branches develop and the leaf size diminishes. Sprays of greenish flowers develop until, at maturity, the entire plant looks like a lime-green plume.

Uses:

When branches have filled out to the seed stage, cut and place in vases to dry naturally, without water. If kept out of the sun, they will dry to a beautiful shade of green, welcome for fall and winter arrangements. Sprigs of ambrosia can be used in gin drinks as a flavoring.

Culture:

Full sun in sandy garden soil. Broadcast seeds over well-prepared soil in fall or spring. Seedlings generally need thinning; extras can be transplanted while they are still small. Allow 12 inches between seedlings. Ambrosia in the seedling stage can easily be mistaken for a weed.

Angelica
Umbelliferae

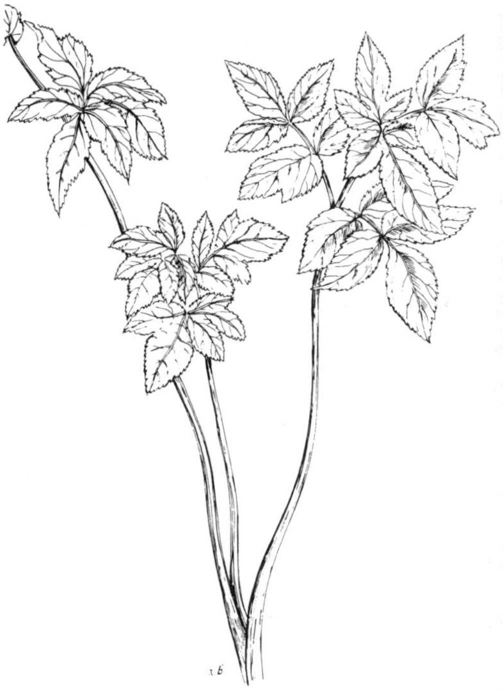

Angelica

Angelica *(Angelica archangelica)* was once used in pagan ceremonies in Iceland. Later it was adapted by Christians for use at the springtime festival of the Annunciation. The plant blooms in some parts of the world on May 8, the Day of St. Michael the Archangel, and hence it was considered a charm against evil spirits. Medicinally, it was used against contagion and for purifying the blood.

Description:

Hardy biennial, grown as a perennial if the flower stalks are not allowed to develop and set seed. If allowed to bloom and seed, the old plant dies, but its place is taken in the spring by self-sown seedlings. Grows 4 to 7 feet tall. Leaves celery-like, divided into three-part leaflets, strongly aromatic of gin and juniper. Flowers greenish white in spectacular umbels.

Uses:

Seeds used in making a liqueur, in vermouth and chartreuse, and as a flavoring for wines; also in perfumes. The candied stems are a traditional French decoration for Christmas cakes and buns; also made into jams and jellies.

Culture:

Rich, moist soil and partial shade in a cool part of the garden. Propagate by sowing seeds immediately after they ripen on the plant, that is, in the fall.

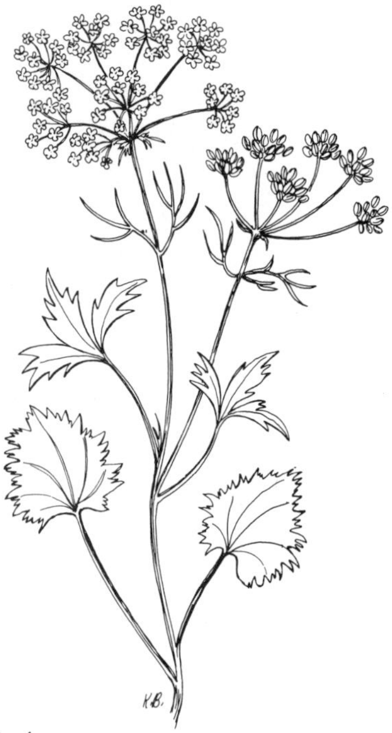

Anise

Anise
Umbelliferae

Anise *(Pimpinella anisum)* was used as a spice in Roman times and was the chief flavoring of the *mustacae,* cakes made of meal and filled with anise, cumin, and other flavorings. This was eaten to prevent indigestion and may be a forerunner of our wedding cake. The seed of anise was thought to avert the evil eye, and in Biblical lands it was used in payment of taxes. The oil has been used as mouse bait.

Description:
Annual, 1 to 1½ ft. Leaves finely cut, gray-green. Flowers white, small, in an umbel about 2 ins. across. The seeds are light-colored, crescent-shaped, with a small piece of stem that clings to them after harvesting.

Uses:
Watch plants carefully after flowers form to insure harvesting the seeds before they ripen and fall to the ground. When the seeds are fully formed, cut heads into a paper bag. Use as flavoring for cakes, cookies, candies, applesauce, stews, liqueurs, and wines, and use to impart fragrance to soaps, perfumes, and potpourri. Use fresh anise leaves in salads as a garnish.

Culture:
Sunny, well-drained soil enriched by the addition of compost. Sow the seeds very early in spring.

Bay

Bay
Lauraceae

Bay *(Laurus nobilis)* on its native shores of the Mediterranean grows to a majestic tree 60 feet tall. The leaves, berries, and oil all have narcotic properties. Oil of bay is used for sprains, and the leaves were once used for a tea. Other plants called laurel, as our native *Kalmia latifolia,* cannot be used as bay. There are only two plants whose leaves are used for seasoning, *Laurus nobilis* and *Magnolia glauca*. Native laurels are poisonous and should not be used at all.

Description:

Tender perennial, 3 to 6 feet when cultivated in a pot or large tub. Elegant, smooth-barked tree, evergreen leaves thick, smooth, and dark in color. Flowers small, in clusters, seldom appearing in the North.

Uses:

As an ornamental pot-grown tree for the garden in warm weather, for house or greenhouse during cold seasons. Use leaves for seasoning in stews, in casseroles, and pâtés. Leaves in flower will keep away weevils.

Culture:

Propagate by rooting cuttings in moist sand and peat moss; provide shade and a moist atmosphere. Rooting may take six months or more. Suckers and cuttings root more quickly.

Beebalm

Labiatae

Beebalm

Beebalm *(Monarda didyma),* known also as bergamot and oswego tea, is one of the few native American herbs used in the garden.

Description:

Hardy perennial, to 3 feet. Leaves 4 to 6 inches long, dark green. Flowers in dense terminal clusters with reddish bracts, the color magenta, pink, purple, red, or white, depending on the variety.

Uses:

Outstanding in the perennial border. The fragrant plants emit the characteristic odor of bergamot, similar to that of citrus. Use the leaves to make a tea, in potpourri, to flavor apple jelly, and in fruit salads. Bergamot oil comes from a tropical tree, not from this plant, though the odors are similar. Bergamot flowers are excellent cut; long-lasting and effective in colonial arrangements.

Culture:

Sun to partial shade in rich, evenly moist soil. Cut back after bloom as the foliage is sometimes unattractive in late summer. Propagate by division in spring or fall.

Borage

Borage
Boraginaceae

Borage *(Borago officinalis)* gained great popularity from the belief that a tea brewed from it gave courage to the person who drank it. The French used the tea in treating feverish catarrhs. Gerard said, "A sirup concocted of the floures quieteth the lunatick person and leaves eaten raw do engender good blood."

Description:

Hardy annual, 1 to 3 feet. Leaves oval, 6 to 8 inches long, blue-green, and covered with fine hairs. These occur first in a basal rosette, then a succulent, prickly stem rises and branches out. Flowers star-shaped, heavenly blue and pink or lavender.

Uses:

Pick young leaves and use in salads for their cool cucumber flavor. Float the flowers in cups of punch or fruit juice. To candy the flowers, cut fresh, dip in beaten egg whites, then in sugar, and dry.

Culture:

Sunny location with well-drained, moist soil. Sow seeds in late fall or early spring where they are to grow. Cut back frequently to keep borage in good condition. If some old plants are dug out of the bed in midsummer, self-sown seedlings will fill the gaps and provide a fresh crop for autumn.

Bugleweed
Labiatae

Bugleweed, blue bugle, or carpenter's herb *(Ajuga reptans)* was once a medicinal plant used for hemorrhage, and it is reputed to have a mild narcotic action similar to that of digitalis.

Description:

Hardy perennial, to 5 inches, astringent, bitter, and aromatic. Leaves occur in rosettes that form a ground cover. Flowers are clear blue on short spikes in early spring. A *reptans* var. *alba* has white flowers and green foliage. A *veptons* var. *variegata* has blue flowers and green leaves variegated with creamy white.

Uses:

Invaluable as a ground cover. It will thrive where few other herbs will grow and may be used where grass is difficult to establish, as under trees and shrubs. New varieties are noteworthy, namely Burgundy Glow.

Culture:

Needs shade and well-drained soil. Multiplies rapidly by means of underground stolons. Solid beds of ajuga need to be thinned every year. Divide and transplant in spring or fall.

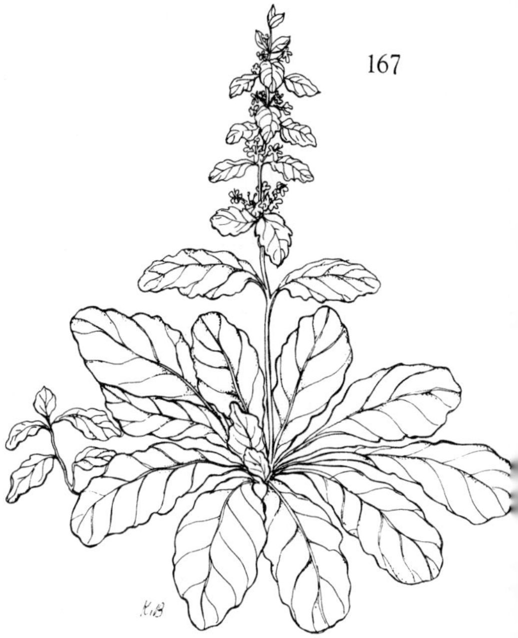

Bugleweed

Camomile
Compositae

English camomile *(Anthemis nobilis)* also known as ground apple, was once considered the plants' physician, as some gardeners believed that planting this herb among drooping and sickly plants would revive them. The Spanish call it *manzanilla,* and use it to flavor one of their lightest and driest sherries. Most of camomile's history relates to its use as a tea in relieving nervousness, for neuralgia, pains in the head, and nervous colic. It is also the tea given to Peter Rabbit after his famous bout with Mr. McGregor. Early herbals recommend it for sleeplessness and as a sure cure for nightmares. Camomile lawns were once possible in the moist climate of England, but our climate is too rugged to grow them in this capacity.

Camomile

Description:

A creeping perennial, about 1 inch high, except to 12 inches while in bloom. Foliage very fine and fernlike. The flowers are white daisies with yellow centers.

Uses:

The dried flower heads are brewed for the tea.

Culture:

Sun to partial shade in moist, well-drained soil. Sow seeds in spring or fall, or purchase plants. Once established, camomiles will self-sow.

Caraway
Umbelliferae

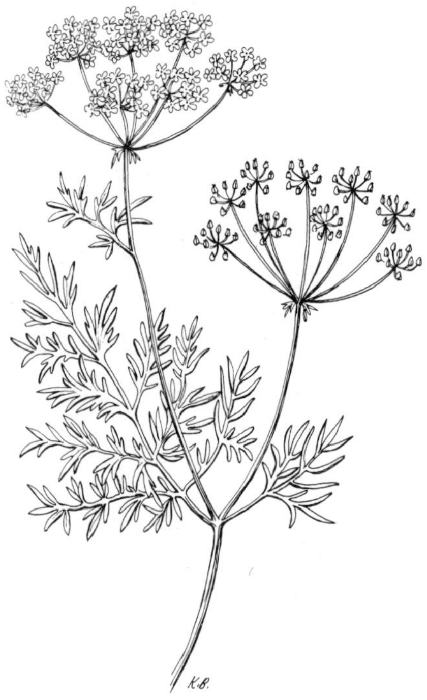

Caraway

Caraway *(Carum carvi)* seeds are reputed to strengthen vision and to confer the gift of memory on all who eat them. They were once thought to prevent the theft of any object that contained them. Lovers were given the seeds as a cure for fickleness, and pigeons were fed them to prevent their straying.

Description:

Hardy biennial, 1 to 3 feet. Furrowed stems with finely cut leaves resembling the carrot's. Umbels of white flowers in June of the second year.

Uses:

Caraway oil is extracted from the leaves and seeds. Young leaves are sometimes used in soup; seeds, in applesauce, apple pie, cookies, cakes and breads; the oil, in perfume, soap, and in making a liqueur called kümmel; also to disguise the taste of medicines and to stimulate digestion. The thick, tapering roots, similar to parsnips but smaller, are considered a delicacy for the table. Harvest the brown crescent-shaped seeds before they fall to the ground and before the birds begin to eat them, usually in August.

Culture:

Full sun and average, well-drained garden soil. Sow seeds in September for an early spring crop of leaves and seeds the following summer.

Catnip
Labiatae

Catnip *(Nepeta cataria),* known variously as catnip, catmint, . and catnep, is a native of Europe, common in England, and an escapee from American gardens.

Description:

Hardy perennial, 2 to 3 feet. Sturdy stems, straight and similar to other mints, square and set with leaves 2 to 3 inches long, downy, heart-shaped, green above, gray below. Flowers pale purplish in dense clusters on spikes. The plant is attractive to bees, almost irresistible to cats, and disliked by rats. Other species recommended for the garden include *N. mussini, N.* 'Six Hills Giant,' *N. grandiflora, N. macrantha* (blue flowers in spring), *N. nuda* and *reticulata.*

Uses:

Cats usually like dried leaves and blossoms better than fresh. A tea brewed from dried leaves may be used to soothe the nerves. All the nepetas are decorative, and they are remarkable in dry weather, continuing to bloom until fall if cut back after the first flowering.

Culture:

Sun or partial shade in sandy or rich soil. Catnip self-sows after it has become established. Propagate also by division of roots in spring or fall.

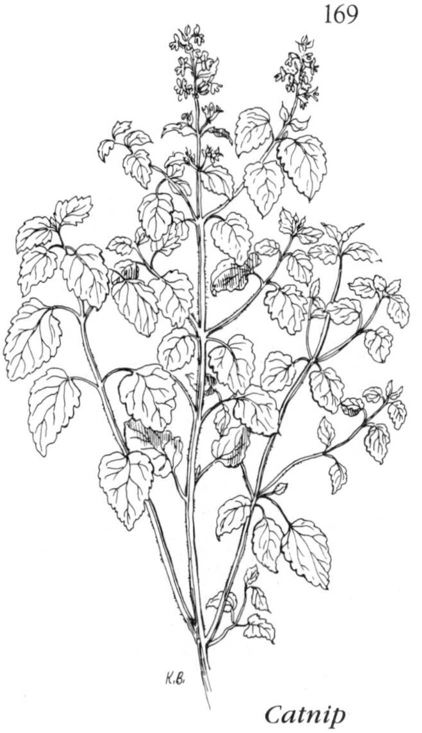

Catnip

Chervil
Umbelliferae

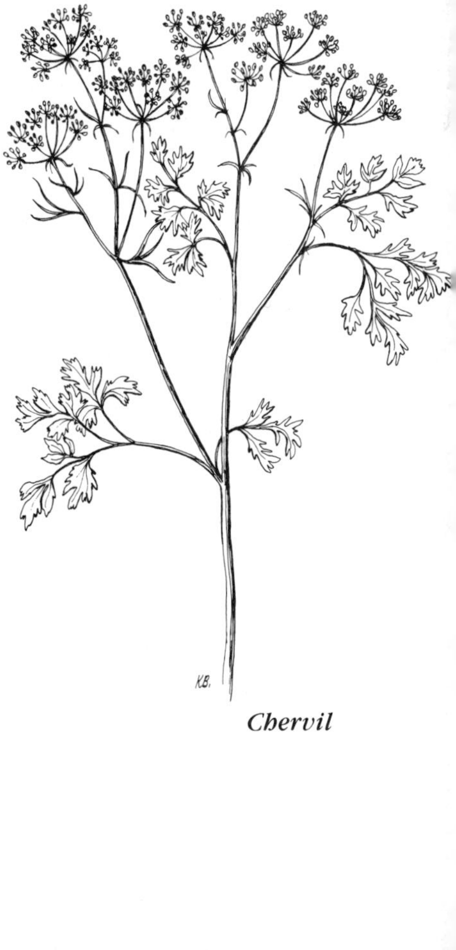

Chervil

Chervil *(Anthriscus cerefolium),* also called beaked parsley and French parsley, is the gourmet's parsley. True chervil is often confused with sweet cicely which is sometimes called sweet chervil. Therefore, when early writers speak of chervil, they mean sweet cicely or sweet chervil *(Myrrhis odorata),* not the plant discussed here.

Description:

Annual, 1 to 2 feet. Leaves alternate, fernlike, and spreading. The plant resembles Italian parsley, though more delicate, and turns reddish in the fall. Small white flowers in compound umbels.

Uses:

Attractive in garden. Use leaves in salads and soups, with oysters, and as a garnish. The curled variety is best to grow as it has the flavor of anise.

Culture:

Moist, well-drained soil in partial shade. Sow seeds early in spring for an early summer crop; sow again in late summer for a fall harvest and one in early spring. Self-sows year after year.

Chives
Liliaceae

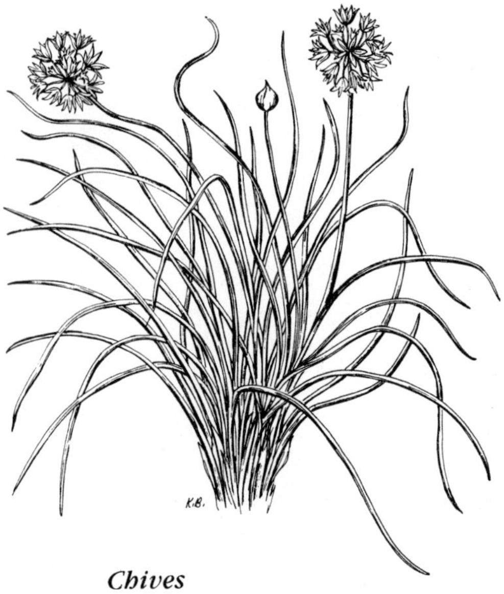

Chives

Chives *(Allium schoenoprasum)* is one of the most familiar of all plants to the herb grower. The plants are cultivated for the onion-flavored, edible leaves, as a border for the culinary garden, and for the heads of lilac-colored flowers which may be used in arrangements.

Description:
Hardy perennial to 1 foot, producing fountains of hollow, cylindrical leaves. The variety Ruby Gem has gray foliage and pink-ruby flowers; another variety, *A. tuberosum,* often called garlic chives or Chinese chives, blooms naturally in July and August, but is forced by florists for early spring flower shows. It has wider leaves than common chives, and the white flowers grow in attractive starlike clusters on long slender stems; very fragrant.

Uses:
Cut the leaves for soups and salads from early spring on; use in cream cheese mixtures, with mashed potatoes, in hamburger, or with eggs in omelettes. Blossoms and leaves are good in salads. Blossoms can be used to flavor vinegar. Chives can be frozen or dried for winter seasoning.

Culture:
Sunny, well-drained garden loam. Sow seeds in spring or fall. Takes nearly a year to establish from seed. Divide established clumps every third or fourth year.

Coriander
Umbelliferae

Coriander *(Coriandrum sativum)* is one of the earliest known spices; found in Egyptian tombs and used as a meat preservative in Rome. It came to England with the Romans and was cultivated in monastery gardens during the Middle Ages. Coriander was brought to America with the first colonists. It was used medicinally by the Egyptians and by Hippocrates. In *The Thousand and One Nights* coriander was used as an aphrodisiac and associated with fennel to summon devils.

Description:
Annual, 2 feet. Leaves finely cut like parsley. Delicate flowers in umbels, rosy lavender, appearing in late June.
Uses:
Harvest seeds as early as possible, otherwise they will bend the weak stems to the ground and be lost. Use in curry, in chopped meat, stews, sausage, gingerbread, cookies, and candies. The seed is very fragrant as well as flavorful and is often used in potpourri. The green leaves are used in Mexican and oriental cooking.
Culture:
Full sun in well-drained, moist, and fertile soil. Sow seeds in early spring where they are to grow, and thin out the seedlings while they are still small. If not harvested promptly, the seeds will self-sow and spring up all around the parent plants.

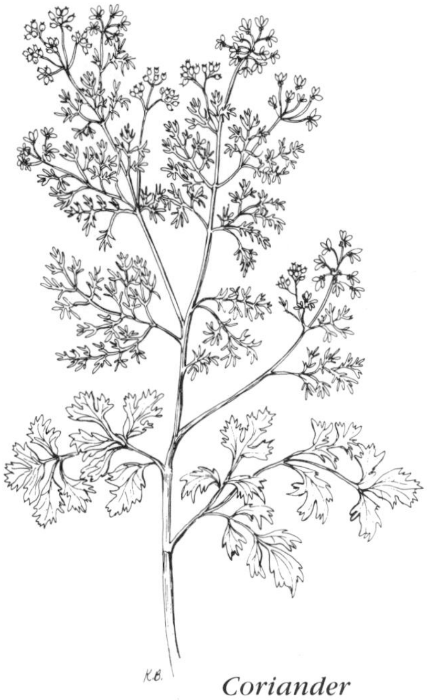

Coriander

Costmary
Compositae

Costmary *(Chrysanthemum balsamita* var. *tanacetoides),* also called alecost, is a native of the Orient now naturalized in our country. The French dedicated this herb to the Virgin Mary, but most of its associations have been with Mary Magdalene. Literature may refer to the plant as either St. Mary's herb or sweet Mary. The common name, Bible leaf, came from colonial times when it went to church as a marker for the Bible or prayerbook, but most of the pungent leaves were chewed instead during the endless sermons, as the minty flavor was supposed to keep the listener awake.
Description:
Hardy perennial, 2 to 3 feet, stiff stems with erect branches, short, and slightly downy. Leaves 6 to 8 inches long with toothed margins. Flowers small, button-like, pale yellow, resembling tansy.
Uses:
Leaf as a bookmark; fresh or dried for tea and iced drinks. Place in closets and drawers, along with lavender, for a sweet odor.
Culture:
Thrives in well-drained soil and full sun, but will grow in semishade. Propagate by root division in spring or fall. Divide plants every third year.

Costmary

Dill

Dill
Umbelliferae

Dill *(Anethum graveolens)* received its name from the old Norse word *dilla,* to lull, referring to the soothing properties of the plant. It has been used by magicians to cast spells and has also been employed as a charm against such spells.

Description:

Hardy annual sometimes classified as a biennial, 2 to 2½ foot native of Mediterranean shores and southern Russia. It grows in the grain fields of Spain, Portugal, and Italy. The plant is upright, branching out from a single stalk with the feathery leaves which are known to cooks as dill weed. Numerous yellow flowers in flat terminal umbels, followed by dill seed in midsummer. The seeds are pungent tasting and retain their potency for three years or more.

Uses:

Harvest dill weed (the leaves) early in summer, then chop fine and dry in a basket, turning often. Sprinkle on fish, salad, and soups during the winter. Harvest the seeds as soon as the head is ripe, otherwise they will drop off and be lost. Large umbels of green dill are used to flavor cucumber pickles and herb vinegars.

Culture:

Rich, sandy, well-drained soil in full sun. Propagate by sowing seeds in the spring. If all seed heads are not harvested, dill may self-sow.

Fennel

Fennel
Umbelliferae

Fennel *(Foeniculum vulgare)* was esteemed in ancient times as the herb to strengthen sight; and seeds, leaves, and roots were used for those "that are grown fat," wrote William Coles, "to . . . cause them to grow more gaunt and lank."

Description:

Perennial sometimes grown as an annual, 4 to 5 feet. The stems are blue-green, smooth and glossy, flattened at base; leaves, bright green and feathery. Yellow flowers are produced in umbels. Florence fennel (*F. vulgare* var. *dulce*), also called finocchio, has an enlarged leaf base which is cooked as a vegetable. The young stems of Sicilian fennel (*F. vulgare* var. *piperitum*) can be blanched and eaten like celery. Fennel varieties with bronze or copper foliage are preferred in the West because of their color, hardiness, perennial habits, and good flavor.

Uses:

Tender leaves and stems in relishes, salads, and as a garnish. Use leaves for flavoring in fish sauces, soups, and stews; ripe seeds to flavor puddings, spiced beets, sauerkraut, spaghetti, soups, breads, cakes, candy, and beverages.

Culture:

Full sun in average garden soil. Propagate by sowing seeds in the spring after the soil is warm.

Feverfew

Compositae

Feverfew *(Chrysanthemum parthenium)* was named for its use in the treatment of fevers, but the showy white daisy flowers gave it a happier common name, bride's button. In the past this plant was located close to dwellings because it was reputed to purify the atmosphere and to ward off disease. It was employed in the treatment of hysteria, nervousness, and lowness of spirits. A tincture made from feverfew warded off insects, and a wash of it was used to relieve the pain of insect bites.

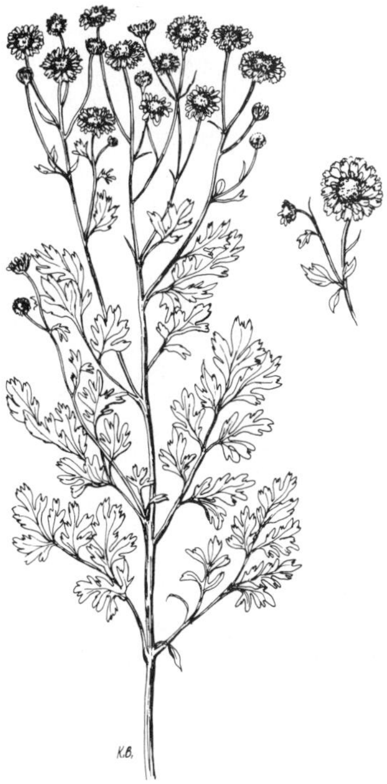

Feverfew

Description:

Hardy perennial, 2 to 3 feet. Leaves light green with strong daisy-like odor. The inch-wide white daisies entirely cover the plants in June. If plants are cut back afterwards to maintain a neat appearance there will be some recurrent bloom later.

Uses:

In the perennial flower border and as a cut flower.

Culture:

Sun to partial shade in moist, well-drained soil. Sow seeds or set out plants in the early spring. Divide established plants every fall or spring, replanting only the strongest divisions.

Flax
Linaceae

Flax

Flax (*Linum usitatissimum* and *L. perenne*), the source of linen and native to all Mediterranean countries, is a crop about which many legends have grown up. Both species have been used for linen, but the first mentioned is more important. The fresh herb was applied for rheumatic pains, colds, and coughs. Flax seed as a poultice softened hard swellings. If a baby did not thrive, he was laid upon the ground in a flax field, flax seeds were sprinkled over him, and it was believed that he would recover as the seeds sprouted.

Description:

L. usitatissimum is an annual, 1 to 2 feet. It has slender blue-green leaves on willowy stems and bright blue flowers. *L. perenne* is a hardy perennial, to 2 feet. The blue flowers open with the sun, wither by noon. The blooms appear in June and July, but young plants frequently have another blossoming period in fall.

Uses:

For color in the herb garden.

Culture:

Both species like full sun. *L. usitatissimum* needs a rich, moist soil. *L. perenne* does better in a well-drained alkaline soil, and best perpetuates itself by reseeding in a soil made porous by gravel and rocks. Sow flax seeds in the spring where the plants are to grow.

Germander
Labiatae

Germander *(Teucrium lucidum)* provided the basis of an ancient treatment for gout. Emperor Charles V is the most famous person to have been cured by this remedy. He took a decoction of the herb for sixty days in succession. It is native of the Greek islands.

Description:
Hardy perennial, 1 to 1½ feet. This plant lends itself to clipping as a small hedge and resembles boxwood. The leaves are small, stiff, and glossy dark green, the edges toothed. Flowers magenta, but best kept cut off so that the plants will stay bushy and full as a hedge. *T. chamaedrys* is hardier, almost a creeping plant, with leaves that turn reddish in fall or when the soil is dry. It makes a good ground cover for dry places and has rosy flowers.

Uses:
As small hedge for the perennial border or herb garden.

Culture:
Sun in well-drained, moist garden loam. Propagate by rooting cuttings early in the growing season. Cover with salt hay in the wintertime.

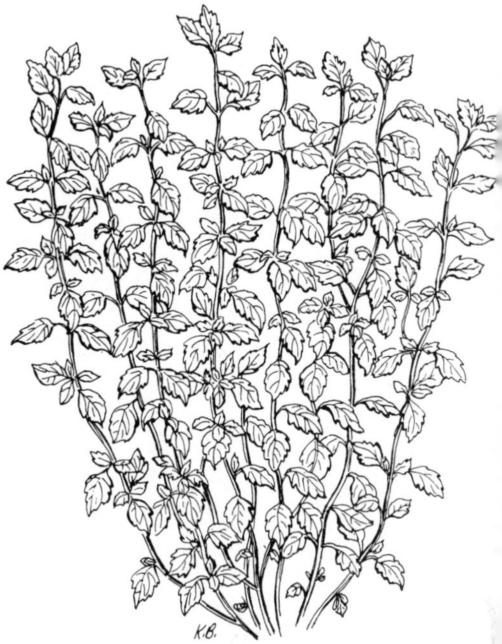

Germander

Heliotrope
Valerianaceae

Garden heliotrope *(Valeriana officinalis)*, also called phu, all-heal, setewale, and capon's tail, is a fragrant medicinal herb. While the carrion odor of the root is unpleasant to humans, it is relished by cats, dogs, and rats (it has been used as rat bait). The root has been used as a drug to promote sleep, to quieten and soothe nerves, to cure insomnia, to treat epilepsy and in heart medicines for palpitations. Asiatic variations of *V. officinalis* were used as spices and perfumes.

Description:
Hardy perennial, 3 to 5 feet. Leaves lance-shaped in pairs. Flowers pale pink in flattened cluster, or cyme, at intervals during the summer, starting in June. They are sweet.

Uses:
As an attractive flowering herb for the back of the border.

Culture:
Sun or shade in rich, moist garden, soil. Propagate by removing sideshoots of old plants. Set firmly and deeply so that animals will not catch the odor of the root and dig it up.

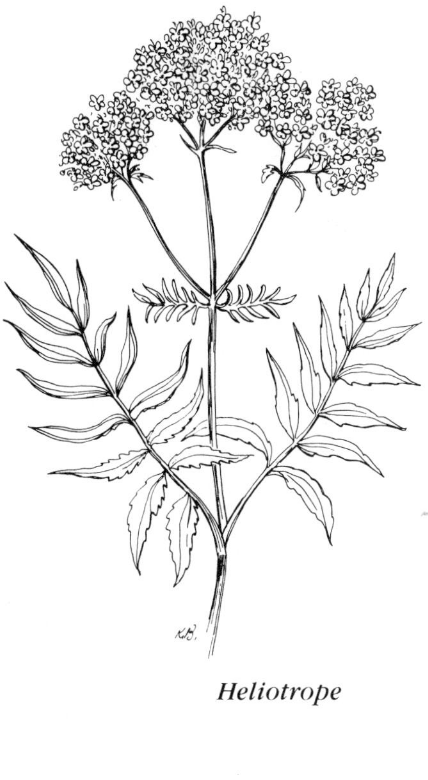

Heliotrope

Horehound
Labiatae

Horehound

Horehound *(Marrubium vulgare)* has been used as a medicine since early Roman times. The Egyptians called it the seed of Horus, bull's blood, and eye of the star. It is an ancient antidote for vegetable poisons, and recommended by Gerard, "To those who have drunk poyson or have been bitten of serpents."

Description:

Perennial, only half-hardy in severely cold climates, to 2 feet. Leaves wrinkled and almost white, forming rosettes in early growth. In summer the plant branches out and puts on a burlike blossom. For best appearance keep the blooms cut off, although in this treatment you lose the self-sown seedlings that are useful in making living, autumn wreaths.

Uses:

As flavoring for famous horehound candy; as a tea to treat coughs and as a syrup for children's coughs and colds. The strange musky odor disappears upon drying.

Culture:

Full sun and sandy, dry soil. Except in mild climates, treat as a biennial, sowing a few seeds each year. Horehound can also be propagated by making cuttings in the spring or summer, or by dividing large plants in the spring. Interesting to try potted on a sunny cool window sill, or in a home greenhouse for the winter.

Hyssop
Labiatae

Hyssop *(Hyssopus officinalis)* was once considered a Bible plant, but recent research has proved that it was a native of Europe and not known in Palestine. Hyssop was once a remedy for quinsy and was used in treatments of colds and lung diseases. A decoction of it was supposed to remove bruises, and the oil was used in perfumes and liqueurs.

Description:

Hardy perennial, 1 to 1½ feet. Plant bears a slight resemblance to boxwood. Leaves narrow, small and pointed, dark green on woody stems. Flowers dark blue, pink, or white in spikes.

Uses:

Sometimes employed as a hedge, but some old plants die out annually and have to be replaced with strong seedlings. The flowers are excellent for cutting. Hyssop's culinary uses are largely in the past as its flavor and odor do not generally please contemporary tastes.

Culture:

Full sun, well-drained garden soil, rather alkaline. Seeds sown in well-prepared, moist soil in the spring germinate readily, becoming sturdy seedlings that transplant easily. If used as a hedge, plant a double row of seeds. Keep the main part of the hedge trimmed, but allow plants on the ends or in an out-of-the-way place to bloom so that self-sown seedlings can replace plants that die out.

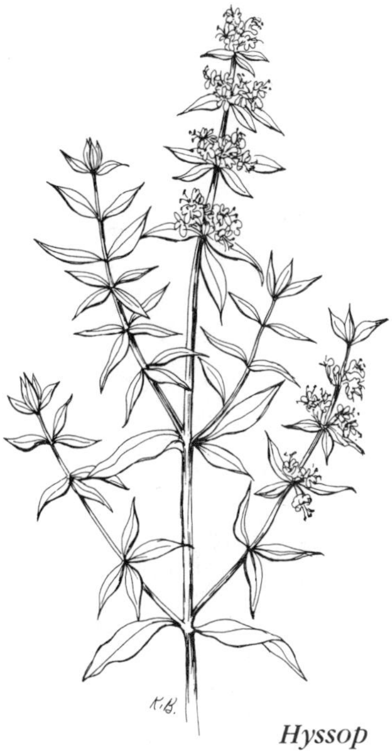

Hyssop

Lamb's-Ear
Labiatae

Lamb's-ear *(Stachys olympica,* or sometimes *S. lanata),* a native of the Caucasus, and bishop's wort *(S. grandiflora* syn. *betonica),* from Europe and Asia Minor were once classified with the betonys. The whole plants were collected for a flavorful tea, said to have all the good qualities of China tea plus virtues of its own. Betony was once thought to sanctify those who carried it.

Description:

Hardy perennials, *S. olympica* to 1 foot, *S. grandiflora* to 3 feet. *S. olympica* leaves are long-stemmed and linear, heavily covered by white hairs that give the plant a beautiful silvery appearance. Flowers purple, in spikes. *S. grandiflora* leaves are rough, covered with short hairs, and filled with oil that gives off an odor at a touch. Most of the elongated heart-shaped leaves spring from the root, large and on long stalks. The flower stems rise 1 to 3 feet with pairs of leaves set on opposite sides of the stems. Flowers purplish red, in whorls on the spikes, in July and August.

Uses:

For flower arrangements and as showy border plants.

Culture:

Sunny with moist, well-drained soil. Propagate by division of established plants in spring or fall.

Lamb's-Ear

Lavender

Lavender

Labiatae

Lavender *(Lavandula officinalis)* came to England with the Romans and found its happiest home there. It was used by the Greeks and Romans much as we use it today: for its clean sweet scent in washing water, soaps, pomades, and perfuming sheets. It was a strewing herb in medieval times and a medicine believed to cure 43 ills of the flesh and spirit. Lavender has always been used to attract the bees and it produces an epicure's honey.

Description:

Hardy perennial, 1 to 3 feet. A woody semishrub that is many-branched with narrow leaves, 1 to 2 inches long, gray-green and velvety. Flowers small and lavender, in whorls of 6 to 10 on long-stemmed slender spikes. There are small species and varieties that make fine ornamental border plants; larger ones can be used for unclipped hedges. Of the hardy varieties, Hidcote is dark blue and Jean Davis, pinkish white.

Uses:

Dried leaves and flowers in potpourri. Oil of lavender is used in soaps and perfumes.

Culture:

Sunny, well-drained, alkaline soil. Difficult to grow from seeds. Lavender can be propagated from slips with the heel attached in moist sand; late July is a good time to do this. Divide plants after blooming. Do not trim in the early spring; trim branches after blooms have been harvested.

Lavender-Cotton

Compositae

Lavender-cotton *(Santolina chamaecyparissus)* is one of the most ornamental of all herbs. It is a native of southern Europe and North Africa.

Description:

Hardy perennial, 1 to 2 feet. Leaves very fine, yet sturdy; gray to white at certain seasons, but blue-gray while young. Flowers, few, globular and yellow, best trimmed off for neatness. *S. viridis* is a vigorous green santolina with a strong odor and interesting bright yellow flowers.

Uses:

For borders, especially in the knot garden, and as accent plants when grown in clumps.

Culture:

Full sun and average garden soil, dry or moist but perfectly drained. Propagate by rooting cuttings in sand or vermiculite. Transport rooted cuttings into small pots until they make balls of roots, then move into the garden. Cut tops back to make plants bush out. Santolina is hardy in central and southern New England, considered half-hardy in the Berkshires, and must be covered in any area if it is to look presentable in the spring. Trim carefully in the fall as santolinas do not die to the ground but come out along the old wood.

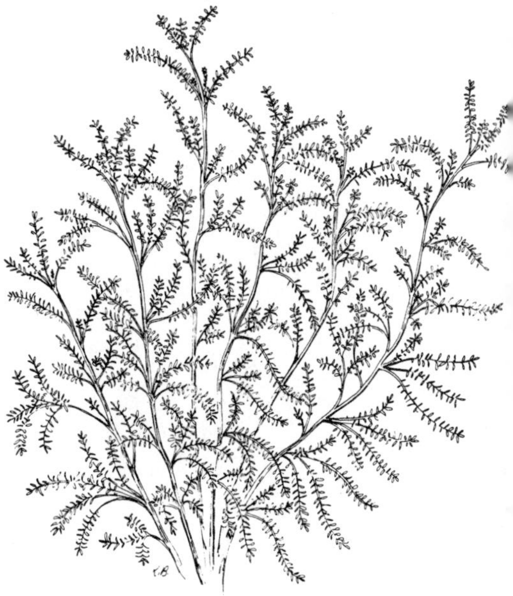

Lavender-Cotton

Lemon Balm

Labiatae

Lemon balm *(Melissa officinalis)* came from the mountainous regions of southern Europe. Linnaeus named it *melissa,* the Greek word for bee, owing to the bees' attraction to the plant. Lemon balm was an ingredient of the famous Carmelite water, and in the past has been used along with honey as a potion to assure longevity.

Description:

Hardy perennial, 1 to 2 feet, with branches growing on a square stem. Leaves broadly heart-shaped, toothed, 1 to 3 inches long. Flowers inconspicuous, white or yellowish, off and on from June to October.

Uses:

Makes an excellent mild tea. Good also for punch, for claret cup, fruit desserts, and as a garnish for fish. The oil is distilled and used in perfumery and also as a furniture polish. The dry leaves are used in potpourri.

Culture:

Grows freely in any soil, but best in a well-drained location. Needs sun half a day, but will grow in shade. When plants are in a flower border, they need to be cut back to keep the foliage a good color as it has a tendency to turn yellow after flowering. Propagate by transplanting self-sown seedlings, or by sowing seeds (germination is slow).

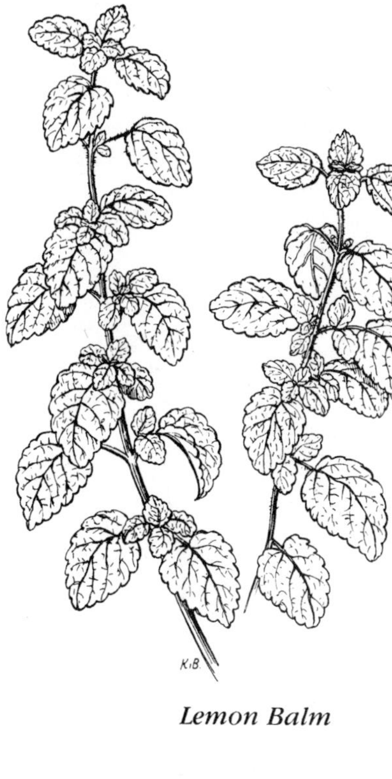

Lemon Balm

Lemon Verbena

Lemon Verbena
Verbenaceae

Lemon verbena *(Lippia citriodora),* native to Central and South America, was long thought to be an herb of colonial gardens. Actually, it was one of the later arrivals in North America. Some say that the Spanish conquistadors took it back to Spain, and from there the plant spread through the south of Europe. In Latin America the lemon verbena is called *herba luisa,* and it is used for healing.

Description:

Tender perennial, to 6 feet as a tubbed plant. Leaves yellow-green indoors, glossy and darker outdoors. Flowers white and insignificant, borne infrequently.

Uses:

Dry the leaves for potpourri and to steep for tea. Fresh leaves may be used to garnish salads, to make jellies and desserts. The lemon verbena oil of commerce comes from another plant called lemon grass *(Cymbopogon citratus).* Lemon verbena tea sold in France and grown along the Mediterranean is called vervain.

Lovage

Lovage
Umbelliferae

Lovage *(Levisticum officinale)* is a native of the Balkan countries, Greece, and the Mediterranean area. It is one of the oldest salad herbs and was a favorite in colonial gardens. The English used it chiefly as a confectionary: coating seeds with sugar. Lovage was an ancient cure for ague; and intestinal disorders.

Description:

Hardy perennial, 3 to 5 feet. A vigorous, coarse plant. Leaves dark green resembling celery in appearance, odor, and taste. Flowers small, greenish, in small umbels; not decorative. The plant turns yellow and unattractive in late summer.

Uses:
Harvest tender leaves for soups, stews, potato salad, salad greens, sauces. Blanch stems and eat as celery. The seeds, whole or ground, make cordials and may be used in meat pies, salads, and candies. Oil from the roots flavors some tobacco blends.

Culture:
Partial shade in fertile, deep, and evenly moist soil. May be propagated by division in spring, or from seeds, if they are sown in autumn immediately after they have ripened. Cover them lightly, and germination should occur the following spring.

Nettles
Labiatae

Nettles have an interesting past as medicinal herbs, and today they make outstanding ground cover plants. *Lamium album,* the white dead nettle or white archangel, resembles the stinging nettle, but does not have its irritating disadvantages. In the past the flowers were baked in sugar, and a water distilled from them was said to make the heart merry, to give good color, and to make the vital spirits livelier. Tincture of the astringent plant was applied with cotton to stop bleeding. It was used also as a blood purifier and for eczema.

Nettles

Description:
Both species are hardy perennials. *L. maculatum,* once called cobbler's bench, has heart-shaped leaves marked with silver and spikes of white or light purple flowers. It is one of the most decorative of all ground covers, long-blooming, and the foliage stays attractive even after the first freezes of autumn. A prolific but not too rampant ground cover.

Uses:
As showy ground cover plants where the attractive foliage sets off white or purple flowers depending on the variety.

Culture:
Partial sun to shade in good soil. Propagate by removing portions of the creeping stems which have rooted into moist earth in spring or fall.

Oregano

Oregano
Labiatae

Oregano *(Origanum vulgare),* also called wild marjoram, comes from the early name organy, because of its use in hot bags as an application for rheumatic swellings. Gerard says, "Organy is very good against the wambling of the stomacke."

Description:

Hardy perennial, 2 feet. Leaves dull, gray-green, oval, with stems often purple. Flowers pink, white, purple or lilac. The most flavorsome oregano is a small-leaved, almost trailing plant with white flowers. It is easily overrun by the coarser types and needs to be kept separate and wintered inside.

Uses:

Leaves, fresh or dried, in spaghetti sauce, sparingly in salads, on tomatoes, in herb seasoning mixtures. Use flowers fresh in summer arrangements or dried in winter wreaths and bouquets.

Culture:

Full sun and average garden soil, on the dry side and always well-drained. Propagate by division of established plants in the spring, by rooting cuttings, or by sowing seeds. The seeds usually produce considerable variation.

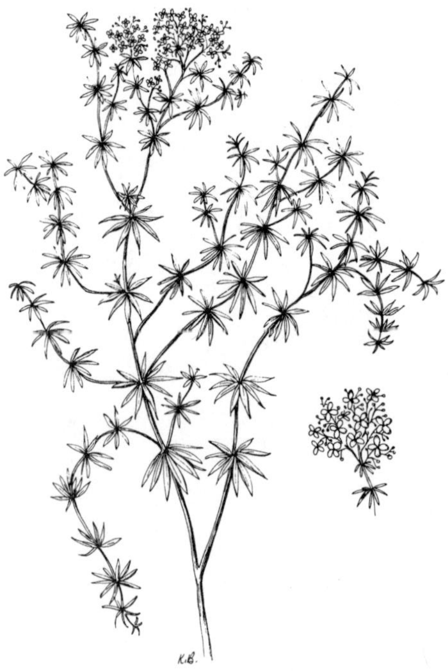

Our Lady's Bedstraw

Our Lady's Bedstraw
Rubiaceae

Our Lady's bedstraw *(Galium verum)* is an herb said to have been present in the manger hay in Bethlehem where it made a bed for the Christ Child. In the reign of Henry VIII it was used as a hair dye. In Gerard's day it was an ointment and a foot bath.

Description:

Hardy perennial, 2 feet. Dainty foliage creeps along the ground in spring; later, as the yellow, fragrant blossoms develop in June, the plant grows taller until July, when the stems become stiff and dry. The small, slender leaves form whorls about the stems.

Uses:
As a filler in flower arrangements and as a dye plant.
Culture:
Full sun to partial shade in average garden soil, even in unmanageable problem areas provided they are well-drained. Obtain plants and, after they become established and have multiplied, divide the roots in spring using the young offshoots. Water well and deeply until the roots take hold. This is a spreading plant and can crowd out weeds. If used as a ground cover, it may be cut back sharply and often to keep low, or allowed to grow until finished blooming, then cut back. Young plants of bedstraw bloom all through July and sometimes in the fall. This plant has become naturalized in the Berkshire Mountains of New England.

Parsley
Umbelliferae

Parsley *(Petroselinum crispum)* was one of the first plants used in wreath making. Chaplets of it were worn at Roman and Greek banquets to absorb the fumes of the wine and thus prevent inebriation. Parsley was eaten after dining to remove the odor of garlic and onions, proving that our twentieth-century exploitation of chlorophyll as a breath-sweetener is nothing new.

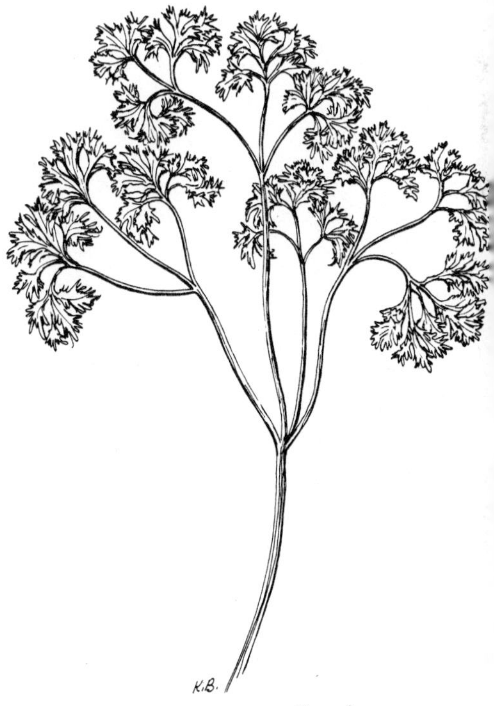

Parsley

Description:
Curly parsley is a hardy biennial usually cultivated as an annual. It has bright green, tightly curled leaves and makes an excellent border for the culinary garden. Italian parsley, also a hardy biennial cultivated as an annual, has large plain leaves reminiscent of a fern which may be cut in quantity for salad greens, or cooked as a vegetable.
Uses:
Cut all through the season, using generously in salads, soups, casseroles, and omelettes with other vegetables.
Culture:
Full sun or partial shade in humusy, moist soil. To grow from seeds, broadcast or plant in shallow drills in well-prepared soil. Sow in midsummer for autumn cutting and to have small plants to bring inside for winter window boxes; for an early summer crop, sow seeds in earliest spring.

Rosemary
Labiatae

Rosemary

Rosemary *(Rosmarinus officinalis)* is the herb of memory which it is said to restore. It also brings good luck, prevents witchcraft, disinfects the air, and has been used traditionally at weddings and funerals.

Description:
Tender perennial, 3 to 6 feet. There are many variations, but all are considered forms of common rosemary. The needle-like leaves vary in color from gray-green to dark green; some are shiny broad, or very narrow. All are thick and without stems, gray or white on the undersides. The blossoms may be white-rose, pale lavender, pale or dark blue.

Uses:
Green or dried, sparingly on chicken, in gravy with lamb, in soups, stuffings, sauces, dressings, in jelly, and as a tea. Rosemary oil is used in medicine, perfumes, hair preparations, bath soaps, and mouth washes.

Culture:
Full sun to partial shade with evenly moist, well-drained, and alkaline soil. Provide liquid fertilizer several times during the active growing season. Root cuttings in sand or vermiculite using 4- to 6-inch pieces of new wood or healthy end tips. Seeds are not difficult to germinate, but are usually slow to grow and require three years to bloom.

Rue
Rutaceae

Rue *(Ruta graveolens),* also called sweet rue and herb of grace, was once used to treat many diseases. It was said to bestow second sight, to preserve vision, and was used against old age, and stiffening joints. Holy water was sprinkled with sprigs of rue, hence the name herb of grace. Arrows supposedly found their mark after being dipped in the juice of rue, and rue is still used in Lithuania as a courting herb to announce engagements.

Rue

Description:

Hardy perennial, 3 feet. Leaves alternate, blue-green, musky smelling, much divided and noticed on erect, stout woody stems. Yellow flowers resembling a cluster of stars are followed by red-brown seed pods that look hand carved.

Uses:

As an ornamental plant toward the back of the border where it will have little opportunity to cause skin irritations, for which it is known, but where the foliage, flowers, and seed heads can be enjoyed. The dried seed heads are excellent for use in wreaths and swags.

Culture:

Full sun to partial shade in average garden soil, preferably dry, stony, and alkaline. Propagate by dividing old plants in late spring or, after blooming, by rooting cuttings or sowing seeds.

Sage

Labiatae

Common sage *(Salvia officinalis),* in history, has been the herb of health and of the aged. An old French couplet expresses these virtues well, "Sage helps the nerves and by its powerful might Palsy is cured and fever put to flight." The Chinese once used it in preference to their own teas, and employed it medicinally for headaches. The fresh leaves were once used to strengthen the gums and to whiten teeth; also it was used as a wash to darken gray hair.

Description:

Hardy perennial, 3 feet. Leaves oblong, gray and pebbly, on stiff stems that become woody and gnarled with age. Flowers blue in whorls with lipped corollas that tempt the bees and hummingbirds.

Uses:

Cut leaves of common sage at any time for cheese sandwiches, souffles, and stuffings. Use dried in sausages, with cheese, pork, poultry, to season stuffing in turkey, and as a tea.

Culture:

Sunny site with moist, well-drained garden soil. Seeds of common sage sown in early spring will produce fine plants for cutting by fall. Propagate in spring or early fall by dividing old plants.

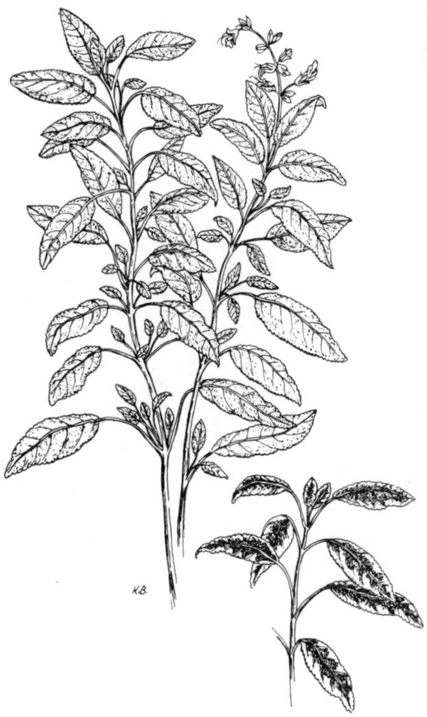

Sage

Salad Burnet
Rosaceae

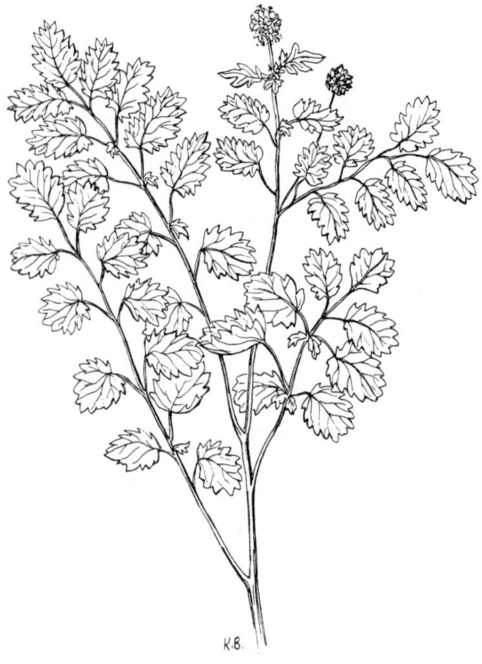

Salad Burnet

Salad burnet *(Sanguisorba minor),* of Mediterranean origin, later naturalized in England and Asia, came to America with the Pilgrims. As a cordial, it was used to promote perspiration; infused in wine and beer it became a cure for gout.

Description:

Hardy perennial, 1 to 2 feet, evergreen. Leaves bear a similarity to those of the wild rose and remain nearly flat on the ground until flowering time. Flowers deep, but pale crimson in a round head.

Uses:

Fresh leaves smell of cucumber and may be cut while tender for salads, vinegars, cream cheese, drinks, seasoning green butters, and as a garnish. They do not dry well. Keep some plants close to the house, sheltered in a cold frame or in a cool greenhouse, to provide winter greens.

Culture:

Sun with well-drained, alkaline soil. Sow seeds in late fall, early spring, and summer to have tender salad greens all year. Difficult to transplant except as a small seedling. This is one of the most decorative of herbs, worthy of space in most gardens.

Sorrel
Polygonaceae

Sorrel

French sorrel *(Rumex scutatus)* is a native of southern France, Switzerland, and Germany. Historically its uses have been largely culinary, although it is alleged to "cool any inflamation and heat of the blood—a cordial to the heart." It was thought to be a source of iron and was once called cuckoo's meat because the bird was supposed to clear its singing voice by eating it.

Description:

Hardy perennial, 2 feet. Resembles the related and common dock of the fields. Leaves succulent, long and shield-shaped, light green in color, sometimes veined with red. Flowers like dock but smaller, softer in appearance, and a warm red-brown color.

Uses:

In sorrel soup, sparingly in salads, as a sauce for beef, or cooked with beet tops, spinach, or cabbage. Cut early in the spring and freeze some leaves for use later in the year. If allowed to blossom, use the flowering heads in dried arrangements. Cut to ground after harvest to encourage new growth for a fall crop.

Culture:

Sun to partial shade in rich, well-drained soil. Buy a plant, then allow it to multiply. Difficult to obtain seeds of the true variety. Broadleaf garden sorrel is a good substitute.

Summer Savory
Labiatae

Summer savory *(Satureja hortensis)* is a Mediterranean native. Virgil grew savory for his bees, and the Romans used its hot peppery flavor before Eastern spices were widely known. Vinegar flavored with savory was used as a dressing and sauce.

Description

Annual, 1 to 1½ feet. Leaves narrow, dark green, on stout stems that become branched and treelike in late summer, turning reddish and purple in fall. Flowers pale lavender or pure white, sometimes with a pink cast, covering the plant like drops of dew in July.

Uses:

Cut two or three times during the drying season, preferably before the blossoms form. Leave some to mature but harvest for good green color from non-blooming plants. Hang to dry in a warm, dry place. Pull leaves off—a long task—make sure they are chip dry and store in bottles. Use in cooking green beans, for all bean dishes in stuffings, with rice, in soups, gravies, and sauces.

Culture:

Sunny location in well-drained garden loam. Sow seeds in early spring, allowing about four weeks for germination. Broadcast in a wide, well-prepared row. Mulch with salt hay to prevent weeds and to keep leaves clean for cutting.

Summer Savory

Sweet Basil
Labiatae

Sweet Basil

Sweet basil *(Ocimum basilicum)* is the most commonly grown basil although there are many others in cultivation. All have a clovelike flavor and spicy odor, some more pungent than others.

Description:

Annual, to 2 feet. Leaves 1 to 2 inches long, shining dark green and pointed. The flowers are white or purplish in spikes. *O. crispum* from Japan is called lettuceleaf basil; it is excellent in salads. *O. basilicum* forms a large bush and is the basil most widely used in cooking; its variety *minimum* has tiny leaves and, if spaced 4 inches apart in a row, each plant will grow like a small shrub. Dark opal has reddish-purple foliage, plants, and white or pink flowers.

Uses:

Leaves in salads, vinegars, spaghetti, soups, with meat, game, fish, and tomato dishes. Excellent also in flower arrangements. Harvest before the plants blossom; cut off flower buds to keep plants producing all summer. Always leave two leaves or a circle of leaves toward the base of each branch; new tops will grow in a week.

Culture:

Sun to partial shade in average, but moist garden soil. After the weather has warmed in the spring, sow seeds where the plants are to grow.

Sweet Cicely
Umbelliferae

Sweet cicely *(Myrrhis odorata)* has been known by many common names including myrrh flower, sweet chervil, anise fern, and shepherd's needle. In history it has been useful in treating coughs and as a gentle stimulant and tonic for young girls. A decoction of the roots in wine was taken for bites of vipers and mad dogs. An ointment eased skin eruptions and the pains of gout.

Description:

Hardy perennial, 2 to 3 feet. The long thick root sends up branching stems of fragrant, anise-scented leaves that resemble the fronds of a delicate fern at maturity. These are downy on the undersides and marked with white spots. The white flowers which appear in late May and early June are followed by seeds an inch long and dark brown when ripe.

Uses:

The spicy seeds fresh and green in herb mixtures as a spice. Use the leaves in salads or as a filling in pastries. The roots may be eaten like fennel, raw or boiled.

Culture:

Shady, moist soil. To grow from seeds, plant in autumn while the seeds are still fresh. Transplant to permanent positions in the spring, allowing plenty of space for the mature plants. An excellent plant for the shady flower garden.

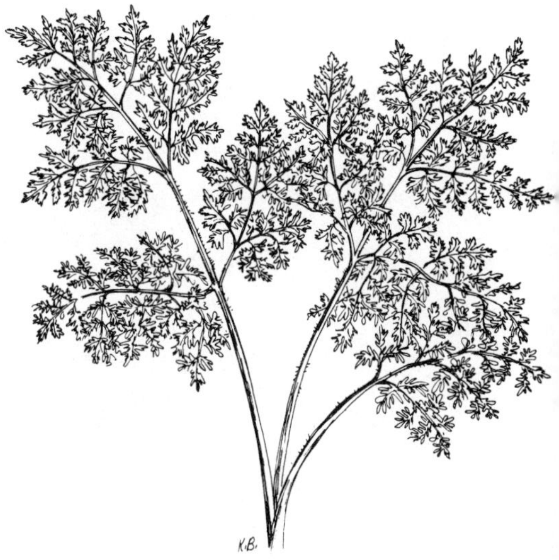

Sweet Cicely

Sweet Marjoram

Labiatae

Sweet marjoram (*Origanum majorana,* sometimes listed as *Majorana hortensis*) was used by the Greeks as a medicine for narcotic poisoning, convulsions, and dropsy. Because of its sweetness it was used also as a polish for furniture and as a strewing herb.

Description:

Tender perennial, grown as an annual in the North, to 1 foot. Leaves gray-green, rounded, and velvety. Flowers in white clusters have knot-like shapes before blossoming.

Uses:

Plants attractive in a border. Use fresh or dried leaves in soups, in stuffings for pork or lamb, and with eggs. The leaves may be used also in potpourri, and in English country places they are brewed to make tea. Harvest the fresh leaves any time. Cut frequently or prevent blossoming. Wash well and hang up to dry overnight, then finish the drying process in a basket. Remove leaves when dry, crush, and store.

Culture:

Full sun in well-drained, alkaline soil. Sow seeds in carefully pulverized soil in the spring. Cover lightly with shredded sphagnum moss and keep moist. Germination may be slow. After transplanting seedlings, water well, and keep shaded until the roots take hold. Cuttings root easily.

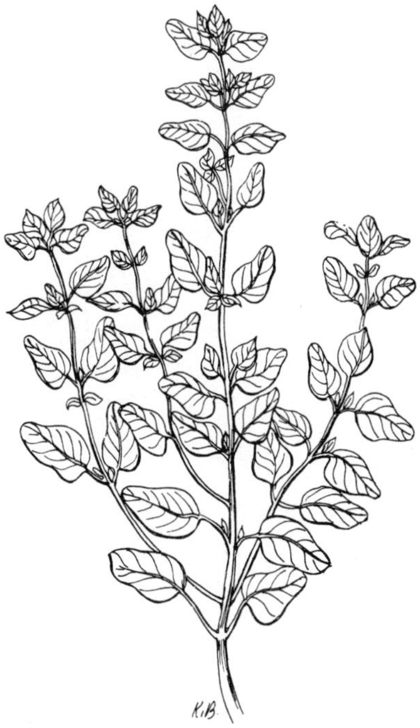

Sweet Majoram

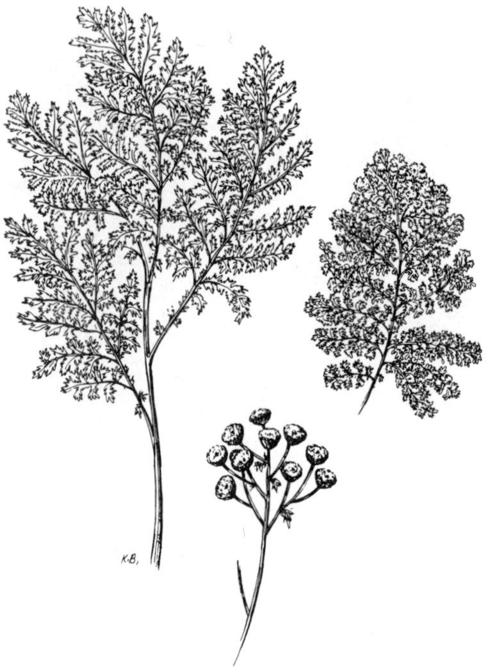

Tansy

Tansy
Compositae

Tansy *(Tanacetum vulgare)* has been called such names as bitter buttons, *herbe St. Marc,* and *Chrysanthemum vulgare.* It was once used as a bitter tea to bring out measles, also in tansy cakes for Easter festivities in England, and in New England coffins as a preservative—or as a symbol of immortality from its ancient use by Greeks and Romans at burials. It was believed effective for keeping away ants and flies, and the large leaves were kept in many colonial pantries for this purpose.

Description:

Hardy perennial, 3 feet. Attractive plant with coarse fernlike leaves. Flowers like yellow buttons in clusters. The variety *crispum,* or fernleaf tansy, is smaller and better for cultivated gardens.

Uses:

Dry the flowers as everlastings for fall and winter arrangements, wreaths, and swags.

Culture:

Sun to partial shade in almost any soil provided it is not wet for long periods. The chief problem with this plant is keeping it from becoming a weed, but if you should want to propagate it, do so by dividing well-established plants. Tansy is best when planted against a fence that will give it some protection from high winds and rains.

Top Onion
Liliaceae

Top onion (*Allium cepa* var. *viviparum*) also known as perennial or Egyptian onion, tree onion, or walking onion, is a practical onion to grow for use in early spring. It can also make a really handsome back border for the culinary garden. Onions were symbolic to the Egyptians of the Universe. Vast quantities of them were consumed by the workmen who built the pyramids, for Herodotus said it took nine tons of gold to pay for the pungent onion.

Description:
Hardy perennial, 3 feet, with succulent hollow stems, ballooned toward the top, and crowned by a head of new plants. The weight of these increases until the whole stem falls to the ground, and there the bulbs take root and form another colony.

Uses:
Cut the spears of the young leaves as they appear in the spring for salads and to use with sorrel soup. Use the bulblets like small onions (they are very strong), or pickle as cocktail onions. Cut plants back after they have borne the top bulblets, and fresh green shoots will grow again.

Culture:
Full sun in well-cultivated, fertile garden soil.

Top Onion

Violet
Violaceae

Violets (*Viola* species) of all types are important plants for the herb garden. The heart's-ease violas were used as a love-charm in Shakespeare's day, as a symbol of the Trinity in monastery gardens, as a medicine for eczema, and the flowers were used in cordials for the heart. The roots and seeds were used as purgatives.

Description:
V. odorata is the sweet English violet. *V. tricolor* is the heart's-ease or Johnny-jump-up, ever a favorite of poets and herbalists.

Uses:
Attractive border and ground cover. Candy the flowers for use on tops of cakes. Use them fresh in punch, in flower arrangements, and in miniature winter plantings where they will provide bloom out of season. Violets appeared in many food and drink recipes of the past, some of which have been revived. Violets are used in May wine along with strawberries, and there is violet jelly, violet sherbet, and even violet fritters.

Culture:
Partial to full shade in humusy, moist soil. Propagate by dividing well-established clumps after they finish blooming. Guard violets closely or they will become troublesome weeds. *V. tricolor* or Johnny-jump-up is a self-sowing annual.

Violet

Yarrow
Compositae

Yarrow

Common yarrow *(Achillea millefolium),* according to legend, was used by Achilles to stop bleeding wounds of his soldiers, hence the name military herb. Yarrow tea was once used in treating fevers, colds, rheumatism and arthritis and kidney disorders. The leaves were used fresh in salads and dried for snuff.

Description:

Hardy perennial, to 2 feet. Leaves gray-green, finely divided, giving name milfoil (thousand-leaved). Flowers grayish white or pale lavender in flattened cymes. *A. millefolium* var. *rosea* (red yarrow) has dark red or bright pink flowers. *A. filipendulina,* 4 to 5 feet, has large dark yellow flowers; its varieties range from pale cream to the golden yellow of Gold Plate. *A. ptarmica* (The Pearl or sneezewort), 2 feet, has white flowers. The dwarf yarrows (*A. nana, A. tomentosa,* and *A. tomentosa* var. *webbiana*) make good ground covers.

Uses:

Flower arrangements, fresh or dried. Ironclad garden perennials for late spring and summer color.

Culture:

Full sun and well-drained soil. Propagate by dividing roots, spring or fall; or transplant self-sown seedlings.